GIANT
of TIMBER and TRA____RT

They don't make them like that any more

Maurice H. Sanders

Japonica Press

**This book is dedicated to my late wife, Helen,
"my forces' sweetheart" who was my inspiration, gentle
critic, memory (after a mini-stroke) and a staunch tower
of loving strength for over half a century**

ISBN 978-1-904686-27-9

Originally published by Cortney Publications.
This edition published in 2012 by Japonica Press,
Low Green Farm, Hutton, Driffield
YO25 9PX
Telephone 01377 270209

Contents

Illustrations

Front cover:

The picture shows a huge boiler bought for scrap by John Evans (for the John Evans story see Chapter Three). Two Fodens, HHT 328 driven by Stan Ruff, and GKX 673 by Alf Hearn, extracted it, as one tractor pulled and the other held it from rolling into the adjacent Grand Union Canal at Tring in Hertfordshire.

Rear cover:

Top: The arctic is the first of its type in this country and now used by Scott's for Timber Haulage.

Bottom: The Foden now engaged in Timber Extraction was originally built for an MoD Trial Evaluation.

They make them like this now.

Acknowledgements

I am greatly indebted to those who have made this book possible. My thanks to all donors of photographs for their time and patience with me, and to Dave Gillow for his usual quality copying and advice. Most of the photographs are by amateurs and mostly directly connected through family or friends with the characters described in the chapters of this book. But I'm also most grateful to Shaun C. Connors, professional photographer and military vehicle historian for his photos of the biggest modern vehicle in the world, other present and former military giants, and the back cover illustrations, the latter reproduced by kind permission of Dave Young, Truck and Driver. My thanks also to Patrick Cunnane of Commercial Motor magazine for his usual help and support. Mention must be made of June Phip and Peter Dorey of the Cummins Engine Co. UK Ltd, PR Department, whose efforts and telephone calls to the parent company in the USA obtained copyright clearance for the unique picture of a Cummins engine for us to enjoy. The "Round Timber Club" has given me great support for this and all my other books and videos. Further details of the Club can be supplied by Mrs Hilary Wood, 1 Maine Crescent, Rayleigh, Essex, SS6 9DG.

Finally my thanks go to my readers, many of whom have become friends through my books some of whom I may never meet in person. There are two, however, whose enduring support throughout, especially in the darkest days of ill-health, has been so valuable – Ben Hinton and Peter Allen.

And if you, my reader, wish to share my thankfulness, please recommend, not lend(!) this book to others.

MAURICE H. SANDERS

Glossary

A.P.F – Association of Professional Foresters.

Anchors – a large sprag or spade mounted on a vehicle to hold the machine whilst roping.

Artic – Articulated lorry.

Cube – 25 cubic feet of hardwood weigh about a ton; this gives some idea of mega loads carried.

Cog – slang for a gear.

Cats – D2, D4, D6, D7 and D8: various sizes of crawler tractors.

'C' Hook – a hardened steel hook shaped like a letter C (that hurts if ones mate throws it over the load without warning!)

DED – Dutch Elm Disease.

MoD – Ministry of Defence.

Quad – a light ex-WD gun tractor.

Queen Mary – R.A.F. nickname give to 60-feet long aircraft transporters.

Splitter Box – a type of commercial gearbox that cleverly facilitates gear changing.

T.P.O. – Tree Preservation Order.

Tushing out – winching out and extracting logs for loading.

Tree Buster – a modern complicated high powered ear splitting machine that converts brushwood to chips and mulch demanding high operator concentration. 'Kwick' Chip is a trade name for a similar machine.

Wind Blow – large areas of gale blown timber.

Wood Pecker – a poor axeman.

So what's this one about?

Ailing health and bereavement really had forced me to lay down my pen which sadly is not equipped with a built in computerised dictionary like the high tec machine that dealt with my scribblings.

Surely thousands of books across the world is enough with three titles into several reprints, and you folk out there have given thousands of pounds to charity and embarrassing limelight to me. To be honest, not all my books have been best sellers. I wrote and published myself a small paperback, "Methodist Memories", with pictures and references to my youth work and ecclesiastical interests to mark the bicentenary of my church and dedicated it to my late wife Helen, solely for cancer research. But it was a flop and is destined for the 'skip'! - probably due to my style of writing and slight rebellious criticisms. Anyway, it is written - A prophet is not without honour, save in his own country'. In fact quite unable to write last year I inspired another three-hour video. Yet somehow at 75 years, in this year of grace 1997 and glad to be half alive, 'I'm at it again', driven on by the compulsion to use the talents I am still blessed with to swell my charity fund, and to extol the 'giants' of the timber trade whose achievements I chronicle, albeit too briefly, in this book. Not only have I been inspired by their example, I have been able to illustrate their stories by some wonderfully unique and mainly unpublished photographs. Not always in pristine condition, they will be a joy and fascination to those who treasure human effort, ingenuity, skill and sheer hard work in the earlier days of power driven commercials - whether steam, petrol or diesel.

To some extent, this book is a tribute to those of my generation who, having served King and Country, invested their time and talents in one of the most dangerous trades of all – timber and its transport.

My atrocious spelling and grammar in longhand accounts for as many red marked corrections from Norman Gurney, my publisher, as my schoolmaster 60 years ago. None of which would have got past my late wife, Helen, who typed every word of "Stories of Round Timber Haulage" on an archaic machine whose tapes had to be wound back each time by a digit as she kept an eye on my written endeavours. Ever aware of my limited vocabulary over 50 years ago, I took up a Readers' Digest plan on 'How to increase your word power', the idea being that you pick a new word daily from the dictionary, rehearse, remember it, then bring it into conversation with dynamic personality change! Wanting quick impressive results as ever, I went for 'Transmogrify', sat holding Helen's

v

hand in the pictures, oblivious of the film as I pondered frantically for an opportunity to use it, so much so Helen queried if I was compos mentis.

The following words once graced a sawmill office I visited. 'TEMPORA MUTANTUR ET NOS MUTAMUR IN ILLIS' - *Times change and we must change with them.* Fear of the unknown fires our reluctance to do so, and for some the word 'Millennium' heightens it. The expression 'The turn of the century' used to mean the distant past but now it is the near and unknown future. Be it seen as dread or challenge, at least change is certain in this age of 'Jeans and Genes'.

Timber historians will remember the century as the demise of our big hardwoods. Ely cathedral tower rests on ten 40 foot long timbers. Something like 50,000 oaks were afloat in the Trafalgar fleet and big oaks flourished across the land.

Small wonder the first Tree Preservation Orders (TPOs) came in the form of an Act of Parliament in 1483, all before 'Tree house top' protesters. When will our urban and chainsaw fanatics who daily depend on various forms of wood see timber as a crop to be harvested and replenished? Do they likewise chain themselves to a Combine Harvester in a field of corn? The so called country loving urban majority have much to learn from the rural minority. Peasants and bumpkins we may seem but actually we are stewards of their bounteous landscape. One new urban immigrant opposite us checked with the planners to see if we had permission to run a sawmill! when they heard Helen and I chainsawing logs. I understand company top management are now sent on a costly course that enables the recipient to learn to relax by not only walking among lovely trees but by both touching and talking to them! So what's new? For yonks we've all said a 'choice' word or two to trees, particularly when they've pinched a saw chain or broken a skid, but relaxation has been far from the result of such words. On the contrary, half the timber jobs would bring about post-traumatic stress to many, and then they'd need that over-rated service of 'counselling' each time a loaded waggon was tipped over.

Hoards of unqualified persons now advertise this service at a price, of course. Fifty-odd years ago, service and civilian personnel alike got no counselling, death was the everyday norm. After the London blitz (a word now only associated with clearing out a room or garage) a network of psychiatric clinics were opened across the city to deal with raid victims. After only ten weeks 23 were closed because no one was attending them, and incidentally the suicide rate halved during the war. Today even police appear to require counselling which I forecast will soon be available 'if one misses a bus' to be followed up by a now fashionable support group no less. Is this a sign of national weakness, I wonder or is it that it takes some horrendous devastation to get our common adrenaline flowing? Perhaps the extraordinary reaction of the public to the death of Princess Diana in its overwhelming grief and outpouring of love shows another and more compassionate face.

In a world where 'human rights' come before human loyalty, where bravado outstrips bravery in a solicitors' paradise, when 'suing' is the 'in thing', changes should be sought.

In the late 1800s a Mr Tilt of Chicago made his name for making high quality shoes and because of their high status he took a diamond shape for his trademark. In 1905 his son equally imbued with a sense of quality products started making lorries. He too used the famous family diamond symbol, placing the letter T within the diamond thus T as a radiator badge. Many of you will remember the high esteem the famous 980 Diamond T Tank Transporter was held in, both at War and Peace: it had no equals in its day.

I leave you with yet another example of resourcefulness and innovation. A big Yankie White artic had been re-engined with a Gardner 6LW. When the starter burnt out and was to be away for a week, a fifty-gallon fuel tank was mounted on the cab top and a gravity-fed diesel pipeline was switched over for the long night tickovers. I imagine the driver having to leave the cab with a torch through the smoke as he opened her up each morning!! What - no Catalyst Emission Catcher? Here I bring you yet again a few more men and women who have triumphed in adversity 'giants' in every sense of the word. In some ways this book title is a contradiction. Because in fact they really are still making them like that all the time and what's more you may be one. I'm thrilled to see those who have this obvious potential.

I once read these words: 'So live your life that when you die everyone will be sorry, even the Undertaker'. Knowing some of the big funeral syndicates, I feel the latter is highly unlikely, and the former would be asking a lot of oneself. However, over the years we've talked about giants of every kind. Imagine an 'Antiques Roadshow' 500 years on. A photograph of an old Matador has turned up. "This", says the commentator, "is typical of an innovative age, a dying breed, then remembered for their abilities to adapt weapons for war to peace. They were a race apart and, as for the photograph, it is priceless."

Your forefathers would be proud to see you work with the vast storehouse of expertise they left you. 'Change' is inevitable. You and I must do our little bit to see that it is for the better.

TIMBER FOLKLORE

Pat Stanley tells me –
Eddie Kite (see the notes on the rear inside cover of Men Mud and Machines) was beside his Foden at 5am one morning when the guv'nor came up the yard and greeted him "You're early this morning Eddie" which brought an indignant reply "Early be blowed (or some other 'b' word) "I've just drawn in from yesterday"!!!

Ben Hinton recalls –
A man had sawn two finger tops off. He picked them up off the bench and threw them to his dog sitting nearby, who caught and enjoyed the snack. Mystified hospital staff enquired about the missing digit tops only to hear, "Oh them, I gave them to the dog."!!!

There's not a lot of folk around of this calibre anymore.

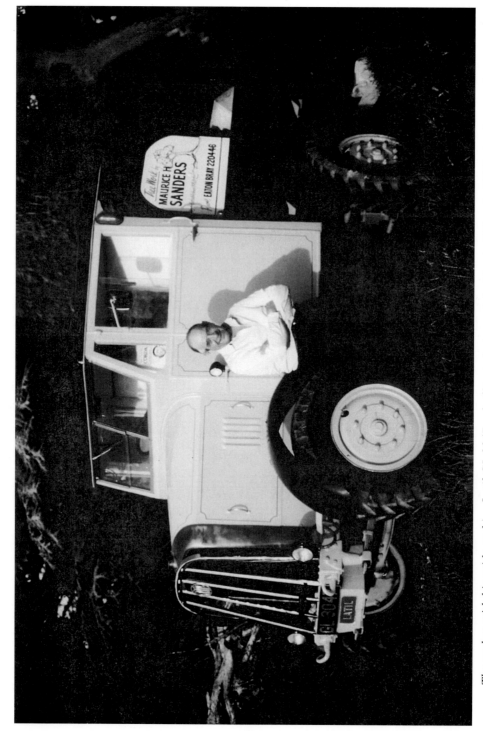

The author with his pride and joy Latil GL 3047, a brilliant photograph by Martin Gillow in 1987 when he was sixteen.

CHAPTER ONE

A real Timber Family

In 1950 this country was awash with thousands of ex-service fellows and girls with civilian workers flooding the job market after five or six years of wartime deprivation. Some of us had vowed 'if only we could get out of this lot we'd not even join a Christmas Club in future'! The promised dream of Utopia was now within our grasp. There's been no unemployment in Dunkirk, Salerno, or Singapore! Joyously we awaited the promised rewards of full employment and free health care for life. The new Britain was to be a land fit for heroes that our friends and mates had died for.

I pluck just two of the optimistic young folk full of hope despite lingering rationing and hard times. Joyce and Jack Shepherd of Milford in Surrey married in 1949. For years Jack was 'at the wheel' of a lorry at war in the R.A.S.C., one such vehicle being a 5-ton Maudslay with a Gardener 4.LW engine, running from Chilwell, Nottinghamshire, down to Southampton with stores for D Day at a maximum speed of 24mph, a long run, shortened by an unofficial plate that forced the fuel pump bar back permanently giving him about 3mph more - continuous clouds of smoke - and a broken crankshaft in Banbury.

It was no surprise that he took to 'the wheel' in peacetime, his first vehicle being an Austin Tipper in 1950. Contrary to predictions, work and money were scarce in an environment still plagued by rationing and national disorder. Jack claims he got into timber by a fluke! A man asked him if he could do six months' timber haulage from Bere Forest, Hampshire, 32 miles up to Guildford. The tipper was swopped for a flat bed 27hp Bedford. Scotch Pine, all cut at 12 feet 6 inch lengths, were loaded up on to wooden bolsters with crude wooden pins. Having no winch Jack dug holes to lower the back wheels. He and the three fallers starting at 6am, pulled on about four and three quarter tons, 130 cube BY HEMP ROPE, and did two loads a day for six and a half old pence a cube - such was the ingenuity of this postwar pioneer, who was set to take knock after knock in a life in timber.

Every spare penny must have gone back in to the business since expanding he got a P6 engined Dodge artic for himself and an ex WD Ford V8 with a homemade jib for

1

Joyce, which left Jack standing as she sped off at 60mph any day! Her mother looked after the children. When hauling from Welwyn Garden City to Sussex she'd be waiting for Jack at Mill Hill Transport Cafe. One day the V8 silencer fell off in London. Neither of them dare stop but when our 'Venus of the V8' refused to continue from the Cafe, Jack explained she had no choice but to roar on!

When Jack once impatiently started winching as Joyce was hooking up he trapped her finger and further disharmony arose.

I think Joyce must have been like my wife, Helen, who'd almost always middle a tree first time when loading. After two attempts at an awkward hollow tree, I got out and did no better and was promptly told to stay in the cab and do my job if she wished me to continue to let her do hers. But I deviate. The war had brought about female work equality by necessity long before Germaine Green's bra-burning theory. Compared with today Joyce wasn't working so they could holiday abroad, buy a boat or caravan, but solely to pay the bills of basic living and survival. Timber hauling is a rare test of compatibility in marriage.

'Publish and be damned' is an expression in journalism and I might well be. Jack left me an action-packed picture against Joyce's wishes which got him some earache. I just hope my solicitor is better than hers. I've reminded Joyce she was not posing for 'Vogue' but caught doing a job for a fraction of the cost that those who do. The 'Catwalk' is a far cry from stumbling waist high in nettles with a three quarter inch steel rope.

House and book-keeping were secondary in the early days. They battled against all odds and we see them buy a new 'Ford Trader' - "the worst motor I ever bought", said Jack. It was for ever stripping bottom gear and finally broke the crankshaft (a habit of Jack's it seems). In fairness, I think a tandem axled pole waggon on 12 x 20 tyres is a bit ambitious with a typical 'Shepherd Load'. Jack claims that the tandem gave tremendous braking power, which I'm sure he needed. In contrast the Trader was replaced by a Commer TS, price £70 - a better unit with limited abilities on hills. Anything over 330 cube on Buxted Hill, Sussex and she'd die on you. Later, two more Commer two-strokes with low speed differentials were the answer. Sparks from the under cab exhaust fired the bankside grass in the hilly lanes like the old steamers did. Next a Ford Custom D800 with Eaton two speed axle D reg gave good service, with a single Scammell axled trailer. Running down to Plymouth docks and back in a day with 380 cube was comfortable until her driver pulled over on a bank to permit a car to pass. The ground gave way and rolling down 10 feet wrote another workhorse off. Hence the policy of 'Thrash' 'em for a year, then replace them. To list a few names - Unipower, many Matadors (one now will lift 150 cube), Bedford, Daff, Atkinsons, one good for 44 mph, loads of Seddons, two speed axles and a fifth gear were luxury indeed.

A major setback devastated the whole family in 1961. Unloading in Bagshot Saw Mills Jack knocked a pin out smartly diving under the load and pole as we all have done. However, the crane driver had pulled the load too tight bringing a 49 foot poplar down off the top on to Jack, by now on the usually safe side, embedding him into three feet of mud which fortunately undoubtedly saved his life. They dug him out and found he had a fractured spine, broken pelvis and ribs, for starters! After fourteen months on crutches, three years later this irrepressible son of timber was back at work again. Two loyal workers and Joyce (then with three children) somehow kept the trees moving and the bailiffs at bay. This, reader, is the fruit of devotion and a real marriage.

There's a lot of dad's genes in son Kevin, one of four children, who went straight into timber from school. Kevin enthused about a man, an innovator like himself who had successfully implanted a Gardner 150 into a CAT D4. And someone else who was glad to get £100 for a boxed up unknown make, ex WD engine which the buyer recognised as being a brand new 7.7 Matador powerhouse that, when fitted, started up second turn over. Now that's what you call a bargain.

A Bedford petrol RL was purchased for a special job. After a 'Hiab' Loader was fitted despite no hydraulic pump drive, due to front propshaft. An old BMC 'Sherpa' diesel engine was fitted low down in the chassis and drove the pump perfectly. She'd pick up 75 cube, and the long chassis would carry 7 tons out of the wood. Now this 'Shepherd Forwarder' was at work in Haslemere when a Customs & Excise officer descended upon Kevin, who looked on with interest. Both tanks were dipped and the official decided to go for 'The Knock'!, saying "You're running part on red diesel". Being shown the 'Sherpa' engine cut no ice and only after seeing the spark plugs in the RL engine did he back off slowly. Now this 'Hiab' Loader was salvaged from another valiant 'Milford Marvel', a six-wheeled Leyland 'Reiver'. In darkness and well loaded, Jack was just turning into a Somerset timber yard when he skidded on mud left on the road by site tip lorries and plunged head on into a tree. The Leyland was a write off and Jack could have been too, as the impact shook up all his previous body repairs.

At Box Hill, Surrey, Kevin has just had 16^1/$_2$ acres of clear fell yew, in Duke's Plantation, the largest yew plantation in the country, producing 15,000 saleable cube, some up to 32 feet long. The haul, a mile and a half off the road, was from the base of a one in four and five incline up the hilltop, tackled ably by Kevin's 1942 Cat D4, which will work a week on 25 gallons of diesel. A Council Forestry official sneered at the D4, then ate his words on job completion. Hoards of crestfallen protestors were powerless since these were plantation trees and not heritage. However, 12,000 young yews have been replanted. Polewaggon and Pain have dogged this family business that has fought the elements and luck of their day. For hard graft and sheer innovation, Joyce, Jack and Kevin have to rank with other 'greats of timber'.

The Venus of the V8 – Joyce in action in 1958. Reproduced by special permission for the author.

The Ford Trader, new in 1961, always stripping gears, but with loads like this can you wonder?

418 cube in this Chestnut with only just over 100hp to take it up hills and hold it back going down. There's ambition for you.

A 6 x 6 AWD of Camberley Thames Trader conversion built for the Indonesian Armed forces (note the two rear propshafts). Several appeared with Electricity Boards and in the Construction Industry. No, this isn't one of the Shepherd fleet, but is slotted in here with her sister Trader and could have perhaps been 'The best motor Jack ever bought'!

The D800 Ford rolls when the road gives way.

Jack says this little BMC 'run about' was a brilliant little motor. Here it gives an idea of the size of a giant Elm. There were two twenty ton loads of timber in this one tree, bound for Martock Somerset, to be converted into coffin boards, and said Jack, "we cleared it all up in a day".

A favourite M Reg ERF with 19 to 20 tons of Beech all loaded by hand. Jack recalls pulling out on a hill and passing a new Volvo whose driver was furious when they both reached the sawmill.

This old Major and Boughton winch just worked and worked and still works!

Jack with the dog and DAF now into illuminated head boards. This was Kevin's artic and well liked.

Kevin with the Cat D4 at Box Hill gradient one in four and five on a mission impossible as at least the authorities wrongly thought.

Glen Hudson looks on, as three generations of the Shepherd family – young Paul, Kevin and Jack are snapped with their illustrious Cat D4.

9

Kevin's ex-Surrey County Council Leyland Landmaster, with 698 engine one of 6 built for export in 1988. She'll lift as much as a Matador. When the winch frequently failed, a Canadian £10,000 hydraulic winch was imported and fitted.

Kevin fills up as he goes up to the APF show at Telford to feature in the Round Timber Club's display. To hire a unit to take a load like this could cost £400+ a day one firm told me.

A load of Yew from Box Hill on the Scania. With 600 cube at £20 a cube it's not quite the load you'd leave on a lay-by over the weekend.

The Bedford RL that flummoxed the Custom and Excise man. From left to right, Kevin, Jack, Joyce and Lyn in 1997.

CHAPTER TWO

In at the deep end

Each of my five books, two videos and audiotape have always drawn kind words from Europe and even Australia! However, a consistent congratulatory letter for each production from an unknown man on every occasion is a record. Helen got to know the handwriting and would say "This is from your fan in Wigginton" near Tring, Hertfordshire, a man who was in turn to become a fan of mine.

A few years ago John Evans introduced himself at a rally which eventually lead me to visit his metal recycling plant, or scrapyard to you, hidden away in a wooded area indicated from the road by tri-axle tyre scrub marks on the surface. John is a big man in every sense of the word. Big, but not fat, with hands like baskets that could at one time bounce, lift and load an 825 x 20 (approximately one and a half hundredweight) wheel unaided. He has been exceedingly big in support of my charities too, not perhaps without reason since George, his father, died from heart disease at the age of 56. At 20 years of age, John and George his brother-in-law were thrust into a business they knew little about. Both had two sons who are now also involved in the business.

I've just handed over a two cheques for £500 to CORDA and Cancer Research respectively, being the first proceeds from the video Glimpse of Horse Power then and now", thanks to the artistry of my good friend, Richard Groom (The Model Man), who donated, with another friend, Pat Stanley, countless hours to this project that commenced in John's yard. Here I'd gathered a few ex T.T. Boughton drivers (forty years on) to revive memories around an old scrapped Foden embedded in bushes. But John does nothing by halves and this unique vehicle of yesteryear was lifted out, brambles and all, just for the event.

The Evans' story starts with father George who drove one of a fleet of 1 ton model T Fords for vegetable growers Mash and Austin of Chesham, delivering fresh produce to Southampton for the ocean going liners. There was a gateway up Gore Hill, near Amersham, that the old Ford would reach before 'engine failure' which was always remedied by unloading a few boxes, manually carrying them to the hilltop and reloading ready for the next challenging ascent. Later he bought a new Ford V8 Lorry for general haulage, and got contracts for transporting Brewery grains from a factory at Kings

Langley. He became very popular with farmers since he shovelled his loads on to eliminate water weight found in other's hopper-loaded vehicles. In the early 1950s George undertook to remove T.T.B's mounting scrap metal, set to increase as the company went into winch and other productions.

Next John tells how they got into transporting the sawn timber from Ercol-owned Latimer Sawmills to their factory at High Wycombe, 8 miles away, sustaining up to 7 loads a day. No time for 'layby lounging' on this job. A well known driver on the T.T.B's giant concrete transportation was a rare character named Tommy Marston (86 in 1997). Let me squeeze in the odd incident from when he worked for John. Like loading, unloading time was vital. One day he was overtaken by one of Whatton's Fodens. In spite of Tommy's use of his splitter box he was left behind. Arriving at the factory gate, he found a shocked driver looking at the Foden now lying on her side! Tommy leaned from his cab with the vitriolic comment, "Don't worry mate, I can get past all right"!

Another day Tommy's load had slipped badly to one side. It seems although he'd forgotten to chain bind it on, his careful sheeting had secured the load to some extent. Coolness of nerve was shown when his overheated brakes had not really failed but seemed disinclined to slow him down enough to turn safely into the factory. With presence of mind he drove past to gain control, turned into a garage forecourt and drove straight through, returning uphill to Ercols under full control. When asked why he'd been seen to go past, Tommy had his reply ready: "I was nearly out of diesel".

Space does not permit the photograph of John's ERF Cummins 220 powered low loader. Many years ago John had loaded a mobile crane which did not look heavy but later was warned it was on the weighty side. Back at the yard he made for the weighbridge, interested to know what the Cummins had coped with. It seems the crane was 26 tons and the whole lot grossed at 41 tons. There's youthful ambition for you!

In the early 1950s many manufacturers officially used ex WD parts, as raw materials remained scarce. Frank Douglas modified genuine Matador parts for the Douglas timber tractor. A popular timber yard crane was the 'Jumbo', based on an ex WD 4 x 4 Morris Commercial. McConnell fitted ex WD aircraft wheels to their mobile saws, in the absence of civilian wheels. Coles Cranes had a standard model they'd built from and adapted to many AEC Militant parts. There was also the elaborate 'Hydracon'. Based on a standard F.W.D. behind the cab was a 3 to 4 ton counter weight (which made a strong case for power steering!). Below this was the usual Garwood winch and lifting cable. However, another winch (hydraulic) supplied jib movement that would pick up a $6^{1}/_{2}$ ton Drott Shovel. But about 30 feet of lowered jib out the back called for much driver concentration on the road with a good helping of red rag on the end, as was quite usual in those days. John made this point very clear. An added advantage was that clever hydraulic motors would slew the jib through 180 degrees because it was mounted on top of a well known ex WD tank turret.

This names but a few entrepreneurs who, as it were, 'beat swords into ploughshares'. Innovation reigns within the Evans' yard which has to include all four of the family. I noted an ex Lister concrete mixer engine, rear cab mounted, was available to fit various artic tractor units supplying tipping ram power on different large bulk trailers where no P.T.O. was fitted on the gearbox.

I've received enough encouragement from John Evans to be biased, but one sentiment must override all others - his philosophy of life: give help to those that need it.

Denis Stacy, Peter Dickens and Denis Lee discuss this, the first Boughton winch in John Evans yard. When previously fitted to another Fordson Industrial tractor it brought loads up from Devon to Amersham with the driver often sleeping under the roadside hedge.

This portable winch designed for tripod loading was powered by an ex-Morris Minor engine and would lift fairly big trees. During the early 1930s a car was dismantled, its body went for a summer house and its engine gave years of power to this Boughton innovation.

All of you who go to health farms will know of world renowned Champneys near John's abode. His father drove this Morris Commercial in 1935 for them.

The 1938 Ford V8 supplied to George Evans – the first of many lorries.

15

John aged 12 years became proficient with this ex-WD CHEV and his father entrusted him with loading timbers etc in the yard.

George and John remove a 2-cylinder, Mirlesses Bickerton and Day 100hp Pumping Engine from Tringford Herts reservoir pumping station.

The unique FWD mounted 'Hydracon' crane. ex-East's Sawmills, Berkhampsted.

New in 1958 this 'S' type Bedford with Leyland engine, 5-speed gearbox, and 2-speed axle is coupled to an ex-WD La Cross trailer, and loaded with father's 10-ton David Paxman traction engine.

This Scammell trailer is seen loaded with 52 14 x 20 wheels – all part of the Evans family day.

A 1,100 cube of plank, being one of the regular loads run from Latimer Sawmills to the Ercol factory at High Wycombe.

How to take nine tractors to a rally! What a marvellous invention the Tri-Axle trailer is. John makes good use of these two.

In Boughton's yard overlooking Latimer Sawmills. The company were agents for the Marrel Skip unit fitted here on a BMC and Leyland Beaver chassis. Later they developed their own design.

Boughton's first production Skip, purchased by John's father. This unit outlasted five lorries it was fitted on, and took 21 years of punishment.

The pride of the fleet today. A Foden 4380 Cummins powered M11 380hp equipped with Boughton 'Ampliroll' roll-on roll-off unit. What a waggon!

CHAPTER THREE

Kings of Improvisation

Peter Dickens and Dennis Stacy both attended the filming of 6 ex-TT Boughton lads, the former giving 49 years and latter a little less. If ever I'm flummoxed to condense two unbelievable lives in timber it is now. I can only scratch the surface of the story of two remarkable men. Peter excelled as a fitter and mechanic and equally Dennis as a welder and engineer. Round the clock calls to numerous field, forest and roadside breakdowns called for trouble shooting a multitude of vehicles - often stranded in undignified positions in spite of their ultra durability and ruggedness but which had succumbed to mega poundings from drivers who'd been set impossible tasks of extraction and haulage.

No professional job title describes the numerous emergencies they faced. Peter was required to have a vast knowledge of a host of machines whilst Dennis seemed to be blessed with abilities to cut, machine, weld and adapt draughtsmen's plans into working reality and make the part which you couldn't obtain for love nor money. Kings of innovation, these two men came up with answers that baffled experts, and would improvise ideas before they could be calculated on the drawing board. With sparse information of what was needed, they would hastily load a truck, drive miles to some defunct, perhaps ex WD vehicle that during the war would have been attended by a workshop waggon crewed by REME specialists. A steady flow of anecdotal memories of men who played well their part in the great 100 years of 'Boughton History' held me spellbound. These facts that sound like fiction sadly are very condensed. Sit in with me if you will and listen.

Boughtons only had one Unipower. Dennis had to take out acetylene cutting gear to amputate the anchor completely, such was the site terrain. A new gearbox (some of you know what's coming) was sent to Peter minus a selector!: a favour for Foden!!

Dennis built 4 remarkably successful mobile cranes based on ex WD Chevrolets. A forward jib prevented the medical condition known as 'Matador Neck'. Axles were reversed, thus the rear wheel steering was comparable with that luxury 'Power Steering' today. A 3½ ton lift was rigged up via a shaft driven Garwood winch, and a manual winch controlled the jib range. He built 4 special big trailers to convey huge pre-cast concrete house sections from Norwich to the infamous Broadwater Farm and Rowan Point estates in London. When a further 16 were required urgently to the same specification, a firm of professional trailer builders took on the contract. Dennis had sited his landing legs far enough back to clear a 6 wheeler chassis. The pros did not! No comment; you can imagine the rest!

A further Stacy innovation comes in the form of an ex RAF trailer with a very long extended drawbar to transport 4 railway carriages 57 feet long, which leads me to the antics of another TTB adaptation - an ex WD Ford V8 Quad which was to add to Middle East petroleum wealth! One duty was towing a trailer to which ex RAF 60 foot 'Queen Mary' trailers, two at a time, i.e. one upside down on the other, were brought from ex WD sales making almost 100 feet in overall length. I understand one 'QM' was fitted with a Marshall tractor less its wheels to belt drive a Stenner band saw fitted at the other end, and went to Scotland as a mobile saw. The Quad lowloaded Cat D6's at 10 tons a time.

On two successive occasions the Quad came up from Portsmouth heavily overloaded with a Cat D6 mostly in bottom gear. Not surprisingly, continuous high revs would put the stripped bolts holding the fan blades, through the radiator. Once parked in gear in a shed, her driver cranked her up, and had to leap up onto a bench and was still clinging on as the Quad ploughed completely through the end of the shed, bench and driver attached.

The Boughton-built, best pole trailer bar none represents so much of this man's artistry. Based on the ex WD 20 ton Albion tank transporter back end, some of these were also collected by the Quad. There's little 'glorious' about Devon after miles and miles on a seat stuffed with horse hair, far removed from the buttock balanced 'Bostrum' seat of today. I doubt there are few places this side of Lands End that are not the location of some mechanical memory of major repairs in what are now environmentally unfriendly conditions. Together with his late brother, John, (see my book "Characters of Wood WurliTzer and Wesley", page 21) Peter tended timber tackle that had been tortured once too many.

On one occasion, snow was on the ground and pulley blocks were secured to a tree branch so that he could remove a Foden gearbox. Dennis replaced it as Peter moved on to a more urgent shout for help. There was a cafe at the top of Amesbury hill. It was on the cafe's car park with no weather protection he drained and removed a sump and big end on an ERF. Another ERF had its diff overheat so much the oil came to the boil and the whole lot was a write off. Overloading was blamed. The timber merchant claimed a measure of 400 cube which in fact turned out to be 600 cube of green beech which the diff had noticed if the driver hadn't!

Major repairs were always carried out on the spot. Out in Wiltshire on a busy road, Peter lowered the sump and replaced a small end bush on Wally Dell's ERF 6LW. Black with oil and dirt, and a knotted handkerchief on his head, quite oblivious of his appearance, Wally went calmly into an exclusive restaurant nearby and emerged with an ornate tray and crockery with dainty sandwiches. After refreshment, Peter refilled the sump with oil and saw the load drive away.

One night, Sid Brightman (see other chapters) just cleared a level crossing in Kings Lynn when a rear spring broke, the bolster dropped onto the tyre, stopping the Foden almost in the middle of the road. Dennis tells how four of them travelled across from Amersham with a lorry load of blocks, jacks and kit, swopped the entire axle and returned police hurricane lamps, as Sid continued his journey just after midnight. A helpful policeman had stayed with them but it seems with an ulterior motive. He was watching nurses in a home opposite!

As for an ex WD Austin 4 x 4 nicknamed 'The Screamer' by the army, it sounded more like a Latil. Peter says one could expect to drop the sump every Saturday morning, again to fix big ends. This is plus every other conceivable and often inconceivable metal meltdown brought about by timber movement. Driver participation is displayed, for example, by Stan Sear, who'd got his radiator and rocker boxes off and on the roadside when a fitter arrived with a new timing chain. **You don't hear about this standard of HGV driver any more**. Today they don't even carry a spare wheel; mobile tyre services are only a mobile 'phone call away.

A whole convoy of TTB equipment headed up to Aberdeenshire after the great Scottish 'windblow' in the 1950s and set up base in an old army camp. Peter went up to replace a Foden clutch and remained there a month doing other jobs over the border. Much of the timber was hauled to Peterhead docks. Some came down south which would take a week to fetch and return, unlike someone who made the 600-mile trip down in his XK 120 Jaguar in 9 hours. All before motorway networks remember!

Other snippets gleaned were about Bedford JPP 303 (see page 40 of my book 'The End of the Beginning') - a Swiss Saurer axle on 40 x 8s that beefed up the back end. The signs of 'Chassis Bend' had them lay the next new one on its side to reinforce the vulnerable areas before its 'Boughton buffeting'.

A 14 x 20 wheel had to be removed with great difficulty in total darkness, the wheel nuts believed to be 'just tight' were actually taking the whole air pressure since all the ring of small bolts had sheered off. Disaster was averted but particles of dust and dirt were in fact embedded into John Dickens' skin and required medical removal.

These men graduated through the school of hard knocks. We'll not see their like again. Indeed, their achievements were legion.

Chesham Broadway, chains tensioned as they did in those days. Little is known of this general contractor, save that he would pull the regulator back and leave it! Also he became agent for the imported 'White' American lorry and you'd sure come home tired if you worked for him!

This photograph is solely for my friends into steam. You'll all know far more about it than me.

One of Leigh de Fraine's Foden's 'coaling up'. An interesting picture of how labour intensive those days were.

John and Peter with the 3-cylinder Cat D6, whose final drive has succumbed at last. This snapshot, taken in a wood near Dorchester, has the following working hours recorded on the back: 8-5, 8-8, 8-7.

Sid Brightman's ERF parked up on Chesham Moor. It's of interest to note that TTBs also had a short wheel base ERF that would rear up like a horse when moving off loaded. I had a spell trunking with this beast and dreaded the loss of steering for a few yards.

Another 'Brightman' load.

John and Peter Dickens collect these two Fodens from Stratford-on-Avon that were to be registered MPP400 and MPP401. (Note the firm's Austin 10 at the rear).

This ex-WD Foden was to be a prototype self-loader. Two small hydraulic winches were to operate cables that ran up the bolster pins and over pulleys. Wally Dell had even been picked to drive it. But the project was abandoned.

The great Scottish storm clear up, Peter, with hand on pick up, leans toward one of the two Fodens on location. Sadly we can see little of the Crosley crane Dennis built up by fitting a Latil winch for roping, and a Garwood winch with cable lifted via the jib. Both could be used at once. This man hastily machined and lined up gearbox parts taken from a scrapped fire engine up the yard, successfully fitted a three cylinder Gardner engine. He made the jib. After it came back home it worked for ages. Ingenuity was the name of the game.

Dennis says "Really it was only a Chev we turned arse about face". This was an amazingly successful crane.

650 cube of long straight fir, dated by the overtaking vehicle.

This Guy 'Invincible' had a gearbox that wasn't! hence it was 'a one off' of this marque, coupled to one of Dennis's special frame trailers.

Sid Brightman's first load on the brand new MPP292. Almost 500 cube of green timber here. Note how the chains bind the upper trees. Sid complained that although this Foden had the same top speed as his old ERF it had taken him three-quarters of an hour longer to come up from Minehead.

When timber haulage finished a new company was set up at Chartridge, Chesham and moved into Motorway concrete bridge beam transportation under the late John Dickens. There were four of these 6 x 4 Foden tractor units, three of which were new. Here Doug Pearcey is bound for the Thames bridge at Windsor with a Mk 7 two stroke. Running out of Taylor Woodrow Anglia Concrete, Norwich.

*Ready for lift off.
These beams weighed
50 tons+, and were
50 to 60 feet long.
Driver Stan Sear tells
me that when you go
round a bend it's
ages before the unit
lines up behind you.
As for police escorts,
if they weren't on
time, you went
without them.*

*Testing one of the
early winches.*

CHAPTER FOUR

Characters from the West Country

George and Barbara Fearn met and married when George was working for Montague Meyers on the famous Chequers Estate near Wendover, Buckinghamshire. Sid Brightman, another great character and one of twins, introduced George to Boughtons in 1947. That horrendous winter saw the newly weds adapting to the conventional old type of living van that was to be their home for the next three years, moved from site to site by a T.T.B. vehicle. So unfolds one of the most revealing stories of the spartan life that timber folk have been called upon to lead.

An International TD9 was George's first crawler. Soon the whole set up moved to Honiton, Devon, where they were to spend almost all of the next twenty years of their young lives, helping to pioneer the great Boughton West of England stronghold.

Devon is bedevilled with steep hills, and the first job was no exception. George would struggle up with all the TD9 could pull then run back down like the 'Clappers' out of cog. One day he threw a track off and continued a further sixty feet on the sprockets and idlers. Then quite unaided he winched the track down, refitted the brute, thanks to more sweat, sense and inbred know-how, than tools.

The next job was at Bere Ferris near Plymouth. His brand new Cat D4 went by rail, and George tracked it two miles to the site on verges as much as possible. Entry was via a hillside bridleway which had become overgrown to make a narrow footpath which, due to bank slips, George had to rope Sid Brightman and his artic both up and down. When wet, George would hold the unit back to prevent 'jack-knifing', such was the angle of this site's approach. When the tide was in, the entry became seabound but with a new 'Cat' on hand Sid waded in with confidence. The bridleway was council owned and the powers that be decided George required a proper track laying class licence. A special tester arrived, approved of George's skills, then failed him for dismounting the tractor and leaving the engine running. I gather George explained the problems of starting a 'Donkey Engine' perhaps dozens of times a day. Our man from the ministry simply said, "I don't understand these machines - you've passed', then disappeared!

The next move was down to St Austell for six months. The friendly neighbourhood farmer came up with eggs, milk and a home-made 18" long pasty that had meat and vegetables at one end and apples etc at the other - a recipe from the old tin mining days.

The farmer employed a strong mentally-retarded lad who once waited by the cow shed door to wallop an erring cow with a stick of heavy rubber. However, the farmer emerged first and was knocked out. Fortunately George was passing and lent a hand.

Bert Stratford came down with a low loader and took the D4 over Bodmin Moor to the next job fifty miles away, then returned for the van. Meanwhile George had to follow with an old Fordson tractor. It poured with rain every inch of the way and George's Wellington boots were full of water in no time. When it got dark he stopped to purchase four bicycle lamps - two to tie on the front bumper and two for the rear end.

About this time Barbara went off to have her first of two daughters. Pushing a pram up to the farm was no easy task, as well as hosing it down before trudging to the nearest village. These two trail-blazers must have been held in high esteem by Boughtons since a Daimler Double Deck Bus was bought and converted into a mobile home. First the engine was removed and fitted into a lorry by Peter and Dennis. Having no fan, the engine boiled (or overheated) continuously until rectified by the lads. One side of the bus was covered by alloy. An entrance lobby was built next to the stairs and opened into a living room down below, equipped with a wardrobe over one wheel arch and cupboard for food - frequently raided by field mice climbing up the wheels - over the other arch. The firm sent steam coal down on visiting vehicles for a small range heater that would expand and tip over the pots (or upset the saucepans). The upper deck became two bedrooms, but the converters had overlooked lining the metal bus top and most of the year one had big aqua droplets all over, and icicles in the winter hanging like stalactites in a cave. In gales, the bus frequently would sway from frightening gusts off the sea.

This sets the scene of what seems like some sort of marital 'Krypton factor', i.e. a test of love for one another and the job itself. A chemical toilet was situated down wind hopefully of the bus and Barbara tells me all water was fetched and carried from the nearest stream or farm, every drop of which had to be boiled on a 'Primus' stove. Clothes for all four of them, plus George's dirty overalls, had to be washed in a tin bath in which they all had to bath. Lighting was via a Tilly pressure lamp. It is difficult to believe these primitive conditions still existed in the 1950s.

The bus was towed on a rigid bar from job to job. George would steer it and operated extended vacuum brake piped to the bus's vacuum tank. With Devon's remote bus services would-be passengers tried to wave them down. George says thirty years ago wherever we parked up on permitted land, police and council officials would try to move them on, claiming the bus was an eyesore, although painted green to blend with the landscape. Yet today, blind eyes are turned to the hordes of multi-coloured old buses which blight the countryside. This stalwart timber couple had to be early 'new age' travellers - only they worked!!

Trigger Bill, a star crawler driver with nerves of steel, and one of TTB's 'when all else fails' characters, often worked with George who says he was always noted for being broke, borrowing and paying back. His motorcycle would regularly carry three to and from the pub. Trigger would be in the saddle and persons not named would ride one on the pillion and one on the handlebars. When a publican had sold his quota of cigarettes, Trigger persuaded him to lend him money to buy some in the shop opposite where they had stocks.

Trigger was quite a ladies' man, with black hair which had an inch wide white streak running from back to front. He never washed his socks or handkerchiefs but replaced them with new ones he'd get from Woolworths. Old socks of his adorned many a wood in the west!

One brush with the law came from 'decibel' conscious residents aware of absent sound baffles in this motorbike's silencer. The fact that it was untaxed was concealed by the owner!

After the council and police asked him to track up the road to shift a fallen tree, Trigger continued to use the road and not the verge to travel his Cat D6. When the decimated road surface was discovered, Trigger protested "But you gave me permission to use it". I believe he was sacked (but later reinstated) for driving not one, but several tracks across a field of ripe clover.

At the dreaded Yetminster site in Dorset, one of TTB's ploughing engines had its winch cable pulled up into the woods by a Hyster winch with a rebuilt drum to take 300 yards of rope. Trigger drove both the ploughing engine and an ex-steam crane fitted with a Gardener 5LW and AEC preselector gearbox. This travelled with the mud saturated timber along some rail track to the loading bay. Nearby a hose was fixed to a gantry to create a kind of 'log wash' - such were the conditions of West of England timber extraction.

One day in the Amersham yard a Boughton-built International TD 20 side boom pipe layer required loading without the jib, to offset the 5 ton opposite side counter weight which meant one track was very light on ground pressure, not a job for the faint-hearted. Trigger was on hand, hopped on and went straight up the ramps and got this awkward beast spot on the first time, much to the amazement of experienced onlookers. I doubt if "Trigger Bills" abound so much today.

Down at Looe in Cornwall another celebrated dual act was slogging away - Daniel Williamson and his wife. She did all the rope pulling out, hooking up and timber measuring. We're talking about sixty footers now.

By this time, Sid Brightman had taught George how to drive and he had taken over Foden MPP 400 and George, now in at the deep end, took these long trees to a nearby railway station with the front trailer wheels more off the road than on. When the railway's crane couldn't lift them, a second was sent for and still they both failed, so then the trees were cut. To get an idea of the times, it would take George 16 hours to come up to High Wycombe with 500 cube or about 20 tons on, which is not bad for a 95 HP 5 LW.

With few bypasses and no motorways, it could take 20 minutes to get down into Frome and 25 to climb out again unless one went in for a lot of 'rubber gear' (illegal coasting). Once George was riding with Sid and one of his enormous 'average' loads down a hill near Ilminster. The speedo was bordering on 70 mph.

George opened the door and prepared to jump but Sid said quite calmly, "Don't, you'll hit the hedge and be run over by the load". George's reply was, "At this speed I'll still be in the air when you've gone past". However, the advice was taken. This was just another hill to Sid.

The story has been told of a Standard car with a broken back axle. Sid went to a scrapyard and turned up with a replacement from an old Rolls Royce! It was made to fit and worked but only after the body was raised considerably for wheel clearance, which looked a little odd to say the least.

Sid was a well known member of 'West Country Weight Watchers'. Mobile weighbridge operators knew and looked out for Sid, as he did them. In the early days he devised an approach that would damage the weighing unit as he mounted it. It was said that the only time another load could pass him was when he'd wave you through knowing you'd get pulled onto a unit up the road in order that he could sail past laughing.

The Brightman twins were very alike, recognised only by some that Sid always drove an artic, and John's Foden had a detachable trailer. Small wonder when Sid had his break at a transport cafe and drove off just before John arrived with his load, a member of staff was heard to say, "That chap's just had one dinner and now is back for another"!

Completing every aspect of timber when John Dickens came back to Amersham, George took over management with a Ford Thames Van and telephone, etc. By then six haulage units and six tractors were under his wing and 17 members of staff are named.

Eventually Devon council came up with a brand new house for the family, three girls and a son, who enjoyed helping George from time to time. Oddly this place had no electrical connections, but a TTB generator was soon supplying light but no power. The very sight of a bathroom and indoor loo must have been like winning the lottery for them!

Enduring these basic living standards for five years in the 1950s has to be unique. George says it all - "Barbara was a hero". Here is another marriage that has stood the test and the turbulence of timber and time - hopefully for 50 years this September 1997. Yet another family stands out in the pages of round timber haulage's history and heritage.

George with his International TD9 in Devon, in the early days before his brand new Cat D4 arrived. This man was to go on to know every timber aspect of the rugged west country.

Percy Marsden prepares to load Sid Brightman's artic. It occurs to the author that Fordson Majors appear frequently throughout this book.

The dreaded Timberscombe near Minehead job, like a mountain side from top to bottom. Jobs like this make heavy demands on both Machine and Man. Here we see George bringing up his Cat D4, ever vigilant of hidden dangers on locations of this working angle.

37

The legendary Trigger Bill with his Cat D6 sharing the blood, sweat and tears with George at Timberscombe. This place got, and kept the adrenaline flowing!

Chillington, South Devon: George is on his way with a load of Elm for Yandles of Martock. MPP400 and MPP401 were both ex-ministry Fodens that had been on lease in Germany.

CHAPTER FIVE

A great Timber Team

Whilst stationed with the Royal Engineers at Newark, Nottinghamshire, in 1943, I had a pal named Cyril, 'a lad for the girls', determined to educate me in this my obvious naivety. Therefore when an invitation came for ten of our unit to attend a social evening at a Women's Land Army Hostel a few miles out at Collingham, he talked me into these previously uncharted waters. Anxiety built up and come the day I considered either going sick or volunteering for guard duty. A 'Bevy of Beauties' awaited us, and the idea seemed to be to grab who you fancied, whether girls or fellows. I worked my way to the back of the crowd as they paired up, ready to make a run for my bike, when Cyril appeared with a plainish, frightened looking girl, saying: "This is Ivy, she's yours"! We were both lacking in the art of social chitchat and just talked about the war and the weather, then the weather and the war. In retrospect I think we deserved each other. Then quite by chance I enquired about her job. She was a tractor mechanic and from this moment mutual boredom and tension disappeared and self assurance took over. Ivy knew every nut and bolt on a Standard Fordson, and so did I, come the end of the evening. Whilst others were engaged in more intimate forms of farewells, I was just shaking hands when Ivy dropped a bombshell announcing she was not staying at this hostel but in digs a mile or two up the road. Gallant as ever, I walked her back, pushing my bike with one hand and nervously holding one of hers with the other. We never met again, but lessons were learned, albeit about Fordson tractors.

Lyn and Trevor Johnson, who trade as Lincolnshire Tree Service, North Clifton, Lincolnshire, live but a stone's throw from this memorable location and I was soon reminiscing about Newark when they visited the Round Timber Club tent.

Thrusting my tape recorder at Trevor I asked, "Have you had any exciting moments?'. He laughed and simply said, "Most days!". Here we have a real family business which I rejoice to feature. All smartly turned out in blue; vehicles, machines and overalls indicating a standard of professionalism that I'm sure has been earned the hard way. The fleet includes 3 Commers, 2 Matadors, a Unimog a Talbot pick-up and two or three Fordsons kicking about.

Trevor started in the trade, aged 15, at a local sawmill, Clark Bros, the year he met Lyn. He was trained to climb and carry out tree surgery by one of the most respected men in our trade, Bill Abbott, Woods Manager for Stoneleigh Estates. Childhood sweethearts, Lyn and Trevor married in 1968.

I noticed the word 'team' crops up throughout our conversation, and this with sincerity and sheer determination has to be the cornerstone of a remarkable enterprise. Their first transport was a Norton motorcycle and sidecar. This had the back cut off to permit loading a chainsaw, ropes or Monkey Winch, with Lyn trying to sit as dignified as possible; later they moved up market to a Reliant! As the business flourished, they had a dream to establish their own small sawmill, to convert round timber into mining sizes and pit props. A saw was obtained and they would cut a bit at nights after a hard day's lopping andfelling. The orders came in and as they say, 'twenty-hour days became the norm'. They would work through until 6 am, Trev (as Lyn calls him) sawing whilst she stacked the timber to meet delivery demands. Then, in the 1980s, as many of you know to your cost, came the Miners' strike. This event was to the timber trade what BSE has been to the beef farmers. A devastating blow!

Although the dream became a nightmare, they pressed on and now act as two separate teams. Trev and Lyn concentrate on the high and dangerous jobs. Although Lyn is groundsman, she has a head for heights and will go up a tree when two are required. Other than that, she operates the 'Quick Chip' and 'Tree Buster', and she can and does drive any of the vehicles. Vicky and Mark run their own side of the show with whatever equipment is required for their jobs.

One particular timber merchant, who was a bit of a rogue employed Lyn and Trev to fell mature larch to thin out. The head forester for the estate had marked the trees to be felled with white paint. Unbeknown to them, the merchant used to go in at night and whitewash spots on prime trees. When these were felled he would remove the whitewash, then all hell would break loose when the forester checked, with the merchant denying any knowledge at all and throwing Lyn and Trevor off site only to visit them in the evening to say it was all a mistake and employ them again. This happened three times before they twigged what was happening.

Another amusing incident was when they were asked to remove a large beech tree in a conservation area near the Cathedral in Lincoln, belonging to a prominent businessman. This could only be done at a weekend because it was necessary to block off one of the roads to drop one half on the road and the other half in his garden which meant roping and lowering each branch. They arrived to find bunting, a marquee, barbecue and an endless supply of booze. It turned out that the client had invited his friends and neighbours round for a tree-felling party in the garden. They had to remove the side over the road first to allow traffic to flow which meant by the time they were ready to do the half over the garden most of the guests were well oiled, which resulted in loud cheers every time a branch was cut but as the afternoon wore on so did the pop. A solicitor tried to do a 'tarzan' act on their lifeline whilst they tried to finish the job safely amidst some 50 or 60 intoxicated professional people. This all proved too much, so Lyn and Trev abandoned the job and joined in!

Lyn told me - and I quote:

If he says 'we'll get this next job out of the way and then go on holiday' once more I'll brain him. Thirty years on, four kids grown up, two now working with us, holidays seem to be days out, usually stopping off somewhere to have a quick look at a job nearby. At least the long hours have eased a bit and we seem to enjoy the work more nowadays. We have done everything together from felling and extracting to hand grubbing roots out.

The variety of work makes it more enjoyable. I remember when we had to fell and remove a willow on an island in front of a large country house. We were not allowed to burn (before chippers) but could use the rowing boat. We laid brush across the boat while he pulled it across with a rope. The last trip I travelled with it, I stood up mid water to tell him it was grounding, at which point he pulled harder flipping me over the back!"

Lyn stops short of any comment made about the ducking!

The TV programme 'Kilroy' concluded that many marriages fail when husband and wife work together but I and others will disagree. On the contrary, the bond often is strengthened.

In this couple and their offspring, pride overrides profit, and job satisfaction is the name of the game. Here we have a family business typical of hundreds of others in our trade, and yet again I have to say, if society is to survive, so must FAMILY LIFE. '

5,819 of these Commer Q4 'Superpoise' 4 x 4s were built at Dunstable, developed and tested at the Army's cruel tank decimating ground at Chobham in Surrey. This one was converted for timber work by Williamsons of Skellingthorpe, Lincs, in 1974 and re-engined by Trevor with a 6-cylinder BMC diesel. The machines reliability impressed Lyn and Trevor immensely.

Now this is naughty, but how else do you lift a 100 cube+ oak, bound for Venables. Roping it to a big lump of top was the only answer here. This must have made 'Colin' as they call this crane, very metallically stressed indeed. (1989).

Lyn works alone with the 'Tree Buster' (or is it the 'Kwik Chip' called Charlie the Chipper) clearing up behind Trevor. Note all the required safety gear. My wife Helen always declared that surely nothing puts you into more danger than wearing all that sweaty clobber.

This platform unit named 'Percy Platform' was built by themselves, mounted on another Commer that has never failed in 15 years (also BMC re-engined) but these are mere facts. This picture conveys much much more, pride, togetherness, and a truly shared partnership. What more can we ask of our working wives?

At Your Service – Left to right, eldest son Mark, daughter Vicky, and Lyn with her Unimog (called 'Mog'). Mog's platform was mounted by themselves and takes just seven minutes to remove or replace. Trevor stands by with 'Percy' 'The Banana Bonnet' as Commer nicknamed the Superpoise, due to its tapering bonnet shape.

CHAPTER SIX

The Wyre Forest

If Ben Hinton sends me a book and it is not about Fodens it has got to be something special. Although an author seldom publicises another's in his own book, "The Forest is my Life (now sadly out of print) by Edwin George of Button Bridge near Bewdley, Worcestershire, is an extremely fascinating insight into the 6,000 acres of Wyre Forest nearby where this man was born and worked for over 50 years. There are touches of humour. One example is of a prankster who bent a tall sapling over, aided by a rope and a horse. To the top of this he tied someone's bicycle. As the horse backed off the sapling returned to its former vertical position. Many wondered how the bicycle got there, particularly the owner.

His first hand knowledge of flora and fauna was outstanding and in his 27 years as a Forest Ranger his responsibilities covered Dormice to Deer, Rabbits, Foxes, Grey Squirrels (those lovely little creatures that decimate our woodlands and are fed by the urban uninformed) - a testament to his woodland skills. He has been involved with every aspect of timber - planting, felling and hauling, and is acquainted with every old forest industry, charcoal burning, basket and besom broom making. He knew the tough women who'd peel bark for tanning then walk 3 miles back to Bewdley with a pack of kindling wood on their heads. He knew the great Kinlet oak veneer, 20 tons to the first branch, I referred to in "Men, Mud and Machines" and he discusses timber uses down to oil sticks 4 feet long in bundles of 50 used throughout industry. With a bit of rag tied on one end, they were dipped in oil and used hand held to permit drips to oil machinery cogs.

Edwin had played and helped in the forest from a child. Horses were his great love and at 14 his first job was to load and deliver 10 tons of coal in a day! Soon he was handling 5 horses on timber work, and tells of a mare bought for £6 from some gypsies. If a butt hit a stump when tushing out on her own, without need for command she'd step one side or the other, free it and go on her way. Another horse would lie down and rest while the men had their victuals, then get up on the command "Come on, Captain". One would fall asleep during loading and need helping up. Edwin remembers the name of every horse he handled, and it's quite a long list too. His uncle was a great horseman.

He'd ride his horse into the back door way, through the house and out of the front door just for devilment. Soon after his death some horses were seen to get into the churchyard, make for and walk round his grave several times then leave, and to this day no one has been able to explain this equine mystery.

Edwin gave $5\frac{1}{2}$ years of military service as a driver in the RASC at home and abroad. On his return in 1948 he became a tractor driver for the Forestry Commission. He'd seen the first International Crawler come in 1935 and the 20 that worked the Wyre during the war. He'd operated the forest's first infamous Danarm 2 man (killer) chain saw, as we called them. He used the last horse there, his own. Indeed, the forest was his life. I doubt we'll see his like again.

During the winter of 1941/42 a forester came round with two members of the Women's Timber Corps (WTC), a division of the Women's Land Army. I've referred to the WTC many times elsewhere. With Edwin it was love at first sight - Betty Williams. She had dated one or two other lads but now claims she 'tried the rest, but got the best'. They were married in February 1948. They both worked for the Ministry of Supply, Home Grown Timber Department, which was under just as much pressure to deliver the goods on demand as any factory. Marriage must have put a 'spring in Edwin's step' since he'd been given a fortnight to extract and deliver 5,000 cube of timber to a sawmill. Actually, he did it in 8 days(!), working unbelievable hours. His wife and the other girl were trained Timber Measurers, working in pairs. One would measure the length and the other the girth. Not to be confused with you chaps who've put your foot in the girthing tape to up the cubeage! Picture them faced daily with dense acre after acre of clear fell trees often laying as awkwardly as possible. Invariably the point of girthing would be flush to the ground and one would require a Tape Sword to pull the hooked tape through. Picture this task being done kneeling in the snow, then holding a pencil to write down the measurements. Betty's first memory is of the blisters from the hard leather shoes!

She tells with pride that she was in the team that had put more timber into one railway station in one week than any other station in the whole country!

They worked beside Italian POWs who always seemed to have far more sugar on hand than the WTC. Nearby in the forest a massive ammunition dump was hidden away. Two engines off the Severn Valley would haul loads in and out. Yet looking back, the two girls seemed to have been oblivious to the fact that even one small incendiary bomb could have blown the entire district to 'kingdom come'.

The sparks from the engines would fire the dry banks. Both Betty and Edwin recall having to carry water some distance to douse the creosoted fence posts which could burn and re-ignite below ground level.

In 1981 Edwin was awarded the British Empire Medal for his services to forestry, and was a founder member of the 'Wyre Forest Society', and helped to pioneer the Museum of Forest Wild Life at Button Oak. This is but a brief reference to a lifelong commitment to the forest - this great green living world, and renewable resource. Trees are our natural air conditioners, balancers of nature. What a privilege to count myself as a friend of Betty and Edwin.

A quick pose on an International Crawler, so very popular for wartime timber extraction. Dog-eared yes, but a lovely snapshot.

Gibbonswell Saw Mill: Vicky Griffiths, Joan Rosney, Margaret Teasdale and Edwin's future wife Betty, front right.

Six smiling girls and one sober gent.

*Margaret Teasdale
girthing a big tree
at Gibbonswell.*

Timber measurers on the Enville Estate in Staffs. Here they measured very big European Larch in very grim conditions. Young Betty is on the far left.

Here Edwin is clearing dense scrub ready for planting. To keep up the RPM the then famous John Wilder 'Multi Master' required an extra low gear to be fitted to this Fordson County Tractor. He comments "A wonderful machine if used properly".

Edwin going down rows of young Norway Spruce again with the 'Wilder machine' clearing weeds and scrub that choke and kill young trees.

49

CHAPTER SEVEN

Timber Haulier Extraordinaire

Bernard Berrows of Oxford is the son of the man who was Latil UK's Southern Area Demonstrator way back in the 1920s. Brought up in a living van as a baby he travelled in a kind of crib-cum-carrycot made by his father, which was fixed to the back bolster of the timber carriage.

I first met and loaded Bernard with my Douglas in 1970. After topping his load with the C hook right over the jib pulley wheel, I was about to throw up a binding chain when he surveyed the load and said "Now we've got a good bed we want a decent log on top"! This was the norm for this timber haulier extraordinaire.

We've all had our one time big load, so did Bernard - 860 cube of elm behind a Matador. But few have consistently averaged 700 cube a load. Timber Merchant, Brian Gorton (see page 110 "Men, Mud and Machines") looked up his records at random. These revealed that in June 1975 (hot and dry, unlike the same month in 1997) Bernard had averaged 732 cube a load, spread over 20 loads. In July that year he averaged 717 cube a load carried on 23 loads, running from Thame or Luton to the Midlands and well the old 'Leyland Beaver' and new 'Atkinson' knew it. Bernard had the gift of scanning round his load to be then packing them on good and tight.

Space permits me to honour but a few more 'Warriors of Wood' under the title of this book, but this man has really established his place, skilfully and safely transporting loads with about a third of the horse power used today.

This old Leyland Beaver would lift up as she moved off, and the Douglas pole trailer would groan. Here Bernard has a cup of tea before putting on the rest of the load!

Binding on the load near Thame Oxon – there's cubage for you! I understand that today, certificates of competence to handle forestry equipment have to be issued, perhaps by some who've less experience than the recipient.If similar proof of 'achievement' was despatched, then Bernard Berrows and his ilk could paper the walls of their homes with them!

Bernard leaving Manor Farm Edlesborough
Bucks in the mid-1970s.

I can almost hear and smell those
back tandem tyres 'scrubbing' under
the load as he leaves.

The Warren Luton Hoo Park. Here in Autumn 1978 Bernard loaded five Artics in one day for
Barchards of Hull.

Chapter Eight

ERF Enthusiasts

I wonder if you remember the first 1930's hand start Foden STG5 timber tractor CBP58 I featured it in "Men, Mud and Machines", page 61. John Wild of Bosham Transport Services Ltd, Timber Merchant and Haulier of Sussex, produced a snapshot of this Foden taken in World War II. His father, Tom, had been forced to take the new vehicle back to Fodens to have the rear axle spring hangers re-aligned, since the prop-shaft was too steep, resulting in the universal joints snapping frequently. After this problem had been sorted out, Tom drove it continuously during the 1930s and the following war years. I am told he washed it regularly in East Dean village pond. (Not a word to 'Green' fanatics.)

After the war, Tom moved on to J. D. Foster of Emsworth and took over a tidy FWD fitted with a 9.6 AEC engine. Later he went freelance timber buying for Fosters. The latter's debts mounted and he finally accepted the FWD and trailer in payment and two timber cutters joined him, as did his son, young John at 15, then in a sawmill at Stedham. Like father like son, at 19 this lad left the umbrella cover of dad's business and set out to seek pastures new of his own. A period of fencing led to the purchase of an old Bedford flat bed, and it all grew from there. The genes of timber in his blood were on the move.

The most striking part of John's life appears to be his appetite for big and dangerous jobs that crop up all too often. He comes over as a 'glutton for risk' yet, like his wife Jennifer, is quite reticent about such feats. In this day of small girth trees he often hauls single butts that frequently and considerably overhang the current trailer width.

John and his wife kindly came up from Sussex to show me their photographs - all 400 of them, many of their ERFs in action. A lot of the photographs depicted challenging jobs. Like 3 Matadors loading a 28 foot long chestnut butt that weighted 15 tons; or a huge Wellingtonia, relative of the giant USA Redwood fir cut in 8 foot lengths, yet still wider than long, so much so, no bolster pin could be used! Another giant Cedar stood only 40 feet from a hotel. Although braced up and anchored to a massive concrete buried block, it still leaned towards the building. The tree surgeon, William Hackman, had to up his insurance from one million pounds to five. The butt was 10 feet wide and 12 feet long! It was never milled since it contained as much concrete as wood. There was over a thousand cube of merchantable timber in the tops, some up to 70 cube each. One very interesting load was a Burr Oak 9 feet wide by 12 feet long, weighing 15½ tons, loaded by two tractors in Scotland which John brought down to Southampton - an 1100 mile round trip - then taken to a famous veneer company in London. To justify the haulage of one such tree, its value must have been phenomenal. John has his own heavy duty 'Hough' loader, which teams up with his beloved Tasker 4 in-line low-loader of 1968 vintage. I queried if this was out of keeping with all their other modern gear. Not a bit of it. John replied: "It's pretty well trouble free, all spares are available and it's just walked through its latest MOT". As he says: "What more can you ask of a trailer that takes such a belting?".

One faithful old work horse now being restored to rally standards is JDD 819N, a 1975 ERF tractor unit ex Chantler Timber, a sole survivor of the 12 which were built, the last of the A series. Its 280HP Rolls engine in that day of Gardener 150s or Cummins 200s, if you were lucky, really did leave others standing. John always carries a camera in the cab; this came in handy when a driver pulled out from his trailer with a bang.

He'd forgotten to lower the landing legs! John once left his loaded trailer in an apparently dry gateway for the weekend. On returning Monday morning the landing legs had slowly penetrated the ground up to their hilt!

John was always an AEC man but he was not impressed with the Leyland take over. When the crankshaft broke on his Marshall he limped home, bought an ERF from a friend and never looked back. John admits to one costly mistake. A timber buyer was sending some loads to Newmarket and some to Gloucestershire off the same job. Guess what's coming next? In John's exuberance he arrived at the western sawmill when a fellow haulier suggested that this load was destined for the east - Newmarket - and a telephone call confirmed it! What a long way, long day, and even longer list of diesel fill ups!

Bosham by the Sea was right in line for the horrendous storm of 1987. When they did at last get through to the yard, all three sets of tackle were lined up but draped in power lines which might still be live. The first call for help came from a man whose tall poplar tree lay across three driveways. Ironically, John's recent quote to fell it had been turned down by the owner.

John met Jennifer in a shop he used to call in near his father's sawmill. They have three sons. Steven, the youngest, is following in dad's footsteps and is well grounded in the timber job. The company have now 'downsized' (a modern term for cutback they tell me) to two sets of tackle on the road. John has the eight wheeler rigid and Epsilon 9.73 loader, and Steven commands the larger ERF artic that has a Cummins L10 290 engine driving through a 9 speed Fuller gearbox, normally pulling a tri-axle bolster trailer. Steven counted the days to his 21st birthday and gained his HGV class 1 licence after only four half days' road training which has to be pretty good, although I wonder if he did get a bit of off the road practice! Even so, this is a real achievement Mum and Dad must be proud of. They've just cleared up two fair-sized jobs in Devon, therefore I'm sure this lad has been well and truly initiated. A gorgeous hand painting of the '8 wheeler' adorns the bonnet top of their Peugeot pick up truck - this unique family business is a great ambassador for ERF. They seem to have found their niche in extracting trees from well nigh impossible locations. Hiring big mobile cranes with small margins for error is not every timberman's forte. All my books feature folk who have earned their place in them and this family is no exception.'

CBP 58: Foden's first STG 5-shaft drive timber tractor in action. The headlamp masks, and officially required white painting of mudguards tells us that this was during World War II. It's known she ran regularly up to London docks and John's father drove without any lights during the worst air-raids.

The ex-Foster FWD re-engined with an AEC 9·6.

Now we see the load and John's father on the right with hand on pin and a look of well earned triumph.

The FWD in Lintotts Sawmill, Stedham, Sussex.

This was a much loved 1966 ERF with Cummins 180 and 6-speed David Brown gearbox. Pity the load doesn't do her justice on this day, I bet she's coped with nearly as much again at times.

This very smart AEC Marshall with 505 engine has a obvious 'bolster pin bender' load, and must have been light on the steering. See how the back end sits down.

John's AEC Mandator 760 engine with the first load of green Beech off the Goodwood Estate. Packed on tight and high.

Now here's a lovely picture: The Burr Oak in Scotland. Prior to completion of the sign writing Jenny, John's wife took a day off from the office to enjoy the scenery and make use of the sleeper cab.

Moving this 44 feet long 15 ton Screening Plant took more nerve than power since it was not fitted with brakes and tended to even push John's ERF about.

It's now Monday morning. This is not how it was left on Saturday!! John says this gateway looked as dry as a bone.

This is the giant Cedar I mention. At Avisford Park Hotel near Arundel, Sussex. Steven has the nine foot wide butt on the artic, and John has one of the two 500 cube loads of tops. March 1997.

Phil Hutchin extracting timber on Sherbourne Castle Estate. I don't think Phil spends a lot on wiper blades and window de-icing on this air-conditioned cab. He has three other Matadors in just as good order. But joking aside, he's brilliant at his job and that's what counts. Note the chainsaw rack.

A delightful hand painting on the bonnet top of John's Peugeot pick up, painted from a photograph propped up on the windscreen. ERF enthusiasts indeed?

CHAPTER NINE

Edwin Foden and his Band

Much has been written about this giant of commercial transport, yet little is known of his hobby, music. Foden bandsman, James Charles, who kindly arranged the donation of the excellent fanfare for my last charity video, has loaned me a book, 'By Royal Command', the story of the famous band and, as keeper of the band archives, has permitted me to quote from it.

The story starts in 1900 with the relief of Mafeking in the Boer War. (Wasn't this the place Corporal Jones tells us "They didn't like the cold steel up em!'"?) The country went mad with celebrations and the village of Elworth, Cheshire, decided on a procession of decorated floats to be led by a brand new Foden steam traction engine. They were invited to nearby Sandbach town providing Sandbach Volunteer Brass Band would travel both journeys. For good measure a Temperance Band also joined in. After much merriment the return procession lined up, minus, however, the two bands. A patriotic publican had offered both bands free drinks. While the Temperance Band had withdrawn in disgust, the Sandbach Band had taken advantage of his offer and its members were too drunk to make the return journey. This so incensed the Elworth folk that immediately a small committee, including Edwin Foden, set up a subscription to have their own brass band. Enthusiasm was such that three men hired a Barrel Organ from Manchester, pushed it thirty miles to raise money by street entertainment, then pushed it back. Other fundraising efforts secured the purchase of twenty-four instruments within a month! These were delivered and unpacked in the Methodist School Room. Here twenty-four would-be bandsmen, few of whom could play a single note, grabbed any of the twenty-four instruments at hand and set off round the village making a most diabolical sound! Edwin Foden and S P Twemlow (also of Fodens) were two of these men.

Proper tuition was arranged, for which the budding bandsmen paid a penny per week, and The Elworth Brass Band came into being. When the band was dissolved in 1902 due to a dispute, Edwin took it over, renaming it 'The Foden Silver Band'. New instruments and proper uniforms were the order of the day. Edwin encouraged the Band to compete in National band championships where they excelled, touring the world as their popularity grew. One highlight was being invited to Windsor Castle to play before King George VI and Queen Elizabeth and family. Steadily the band rose to ultimate fame at the highest level.

One day, in 1940, in this country's 'lowest hour', the band was giving a concert at a southern resort just as the Dunkirk evacuation had begun. The stream of wounded, dejected and pitiable men deeply moved some of the bandsmen who returned to their twelve-hour day of war effort determined to redouble their output. On 23rd May 1945, five days before VE day, at ENSA headquarters in Drury Lane, London, twenty-seven men, groggy from inoculations, set off and boarded a naval landing craft with their famous 1933 bus named 'Bandmaster', made a choppy crossing to France, travelled 2,000 miles across Belgium and Holland giving impromptu performances in hospitals, camps, etc and three proper concerts a day. Here they saw the weapons, lorries and tanks they'd help make; here were the men who'd brought victory with them, a great honour for this now most prestigious band.

With permission, I now quote directly from "By Royal Command" - part of Chapter X, on the Band's Transport.

"One of the problems facing any band is the transportation of players and instruments to engagements but in this connection Fodens Motor Works Band has been fortunate in that the parent company, as a leading vehicle manufacturer, has provided units as required.

In the early days a loose closed body, which could be bolted to any available chassis, was provided, access being gained by a step-ladder which the last passenger on board pulled into the doorway. Although of rudimentary design, in fact little more than a large garden shed, its limited facilities were better than those available when travelling on an open wagon!

As the band's fame grew it was decided that it should have its own bus, vehicle number 4364 being allocated. The unit, basically a Foden three ton steam wagon chassis, was modified to incorporate a five ton boiler and engine, the latter being a two cylinder compound with a four inch diameter high-pressure cylinder and a six and three-quarter inch diameter low pressure one, power being transmitted to the rear axle by chain drive and giving a maximum road speed of twelve miles per hour. The driver's cab roof extended forward, enclosing the chimney top, and was streamlined although this must have been for aesthetic reasons as at maximum speed the effect on air resistance would have been negligible. The special body, supplied and fitted by Jacksons of Smallwood, had a gallery at the rear where passengers could disport themselves in the open air. The complete vehicle, painted red and lined in black and gold, bearing the name "Puffing Billy" on a polished brass plate fitted to the smokebox, presented a superb piece of workmanship when it entered service in 1914 with the registration number M 6359.

The first outing, to Knutsford May Day, was also used as a test run with Mr Jackson, who had built the body, travelling on the gallery to check that all was in order. In leaning over the rail he inadvertently dislodged one of the instruments which fell into the roadside verge, causing a delay while the vehicle was halted and the missing flugel horn retrieved. E. R. Foden, travelling on the footplate in order to carry out fuel consumption tests, found his carefully measured charged of coal wasted and the calculations ruined. His comments on the unnecessary hold up do not bear repetition!... (When the company) changed over to diesel power the directors authorised the building of a new bus and in 1933 vehicle number 15284 reg number AMA 271 entered service. As built the vehicle was powered by a Gardner 4LW engine driving through a Foden four-speed gearbox but this was later changed to a Gardner 5LW and Foden five-speed gearbox configuration. The body was built in the company's workshops and the whole was finished in blue and cream with lettering in red and gold. The bus received the name "Bandmaster" which was painted on the luggage boot door although the author thought that, being so lettered, this must surely be a special compartment in which F. Mortimer travelled!

Sent as an exhibit to the 1933 Scottish Motor Show, the bus came into collision with a Glasgow tramcar causing damage to both vehicles and although the ensuring altercation between the two drivers ended with honours even, the bus came off best in that it was driven on to Kelvin Hall whereas the tramcar had to be towed to its depot. With the show due to open there was no time to carry out repairs to "Bandmaster" but the problem was solved by the purchase of a large Union Jack which was draped over the damaged area.

After the show the bus, suitable for both short and long distance journeys, began its service with the band which continued until it was replaced during 1951 when it had travelled 83,290 miles.

Retirement from band duties did not terminate its useful life as, overhauled and repainted, it operated for a while as the company's welfare bus before being sold to an enthusiast whose intention was to restore it to the original condition. Sadly, this did not happen and "Bandmaster" followed its predecessor "Puffing Billy" to the scrapyard.

The third and present band bus (in 1977), which entered service in 1951, was of revolutionary concept when produced, the company having recently introduced the first rear-engined units one of which, vehicle number 31234 was allocated to the band. The vehicle is powered by a Foden FD6 two-stroke supercharged engine, mounted transversely across the chassis, driving through a Foden five-speed gearbox and capable of producing a sustained speed of seventy miles per hour, a far cry from that achieved by "Puffing Billy". Plaxtons of Scarborough supplied and fitted the body, the complete vehicle being finished in a livery of blue and cream with gold and black lettering, fashion dictating a style less flamboyant than the Gothic script applied to "Bandmaster". Registered as number OLG 855 the bus has travelled extensively both at home and overseas, having covered a total distance in excess of a quarter of a million miles."

As a child I remember the name of Fred Mortimer being coupled with Luton Red Cross Band. It appears this bandmaster had taken this band into becoming the first southern band to win the national brass band championships in 1923. From then on Fred came into national brass band limelight. When the vacancy occurred he applied for and got the position of what was to be the rest of his life's work - musical director for 29 years of the blossoming Foden Motor Works Band. With his three sons, all with great musical ability, he lead the band to win contest after contest, and gave his all until he died in 1963 aged 73.

To quote from a lengthy obituary in the 'Luton News': "This is a great blow. This man has won every kind of contest to be won. His abilities have made him a household name wherever brass bands are found". I heard the band play live only once. In the 1970s when Fodens sponsored the London to Brighton historic commercial vehicle run, two 'Haulmaster' tractors with curtain wagon trailers stood side by side on the promenade making the perfect mobile bandstand from which the band played throughout''.

1913

Puffing Billy

1933

Bandmaster on loan to
Sunday School

Inset: Radiator filler cap from
bandmaster with model of
F. Motimer

1951

BAND BUSES *reproduced from "By Royal Command"*

Chapter Ten

The Round Timber Club

The Round Timber Club (RTC) was formed in 1992 at the worst possible time in the depth of the recession. I saw a need for some ongoing society to promote a common interest that had blossomed among timber folk throughout my books. This dream was made a reality by one Tim Beaven and the ensuing Cranleigh rally was out of this world(!) and followed up by excellent turn outs at many other locations. But plans for the Club's very own show "A Day of Timber Nostalgia" on 17th May 1997 at Merrist Wood, Guildford, seemed to me to be over ambitious. A brave little team under the Show chairmanship of Kevin Shepherd, club Secretary, Hilary Wood, and Phil Wallace (an experienced rally organiser) together with several helpers overcame expected and unexpected problems as is often the case in their daily lives with timber. Ben Hinton with son-in-law, Tony Wall, whisked me down to this function of mind-blowing proportions.

As for me, it was VIP treatment from the moment Lyn Shepherd on radio traffic control guided us in until the fond farewells. Equipment from the early 1900s was on show, much at work, and must have astonished eager members of the public who have not the slightest clue as to what our trade entails. A most joyous moment for me was being lifted up into Brian Wood's Hannibal and being taken around the show ground with the 'five potter' at the tick over. I thought of the late Bill Wood who did so much for the club at its inception, how proud he'd have been to see this, his family, in one of its finest hours. For once the show did not coincide with a 'Wood family' increase. Hilary brought her own creche though, in the form of her mum and dad. We all owe much to this young lady who `drives the club in the fast lane' so much of the time.

It was humbling to be greeted with "I've got all your books" so many times. Friends had come from Cornwall, Norfolk, Lincolnshire, Wales, Scotland and even Ireland. Included were members of the 'old brigade' - Reg Hannis (droll as ever), Doug Stemp and Lionel Amos, who'd driven his latest big Foden up from Gloucestershire. A whole gang of ex B J Davies lads from Bucknell, Salop, recalled memories some of the young ones would never believe. It was good to see real good-sized timber being loaded instead of a few poles. It was just as exciting to see Richard Groom with his radio controlled model Loader and Scania in action. His dexterity beggars belief. It was very thrilling to see my old Latil in action again - unique in that I drove her round the Silverstone track taking Woodcote corner without changing down, unlike Damon Hill! The event was 'Motor 100' in May 1985. I'd been asked to give timber loading demonstrations there. This vehicle helped remove the 5,000 trees along the line of the proposed M1 from St Albans to Dunchurch in 1958. Whattons of Hartwell, Northants, were the main contractors for this length. Well done Barry Taylor. She looks great.

To see groups of folk meeting up and going over old times was very rewarding for me. A sad story came from a man who had several acres of now dead Ash trees, due to the lowered water table from 4 years of drought. None were mature enough for milling and were only fit for logs. A listener predicted by the year 2000 we'd need long chainsaw bars, and big bandmills to deal with resultant climate changes, a grim thought indeed. Three times recently TV news documentaries have featured cracked reservoirs and woeful stories of national water shortages, then within seconds a weather forecaster would come on saying, "Hopefully the rain will not reach us" or "I'm afraid there could be rain later" and add, with a sickly grin, "I suppose the farmers need it", when we all need it.

"Repair leaking pipes" they rightly shout with scant concern as to whether there is any water in them to leak. After the first drizzle for weeks, a lady met me with "What a dreadful morning!" Enraged, I replied, "If you've got a substitute for water, you're the world's richest person". "But how can you have a drought in winter?", she continued. Joined by another seemingly intelligent lady to whom the drizzle had given the chance to get her green wellies out, one of them questioned why a birch tree was dying. "Thirst, Ladies, THIRST!". How bad have things to get before rain is accepted as good weather, and dry is bad.

When I was a boy an old song ran 'You don't miss the water till the well runs dry' and we 'South of the Trent' as they used to say, well might come to know.

I digress yet again, so back to Merrist Wood. As well as old friends, I had the joy of meeting new ones too and the name 'Cummins' engines kept cropping up, hence a little delve into this marque for a moment. In 1913 Clessie Cummins started his Machine Works in Columbus, Indiana, USA. It was in the garage of a local banker he had been chauffeur to. His interest was in experimental and development jobs, a man of ideas. The banker backed him and he purchased the manufacturing rights of the HVID engine. In April 1919 Clessie founded the Cummins Engine Company. Four assistants helped design and make a 6 b.h.p. single cylinder, kerosene engine. A mail order firm ordered 4,500 of various b.h.p., put a money back guarantee on the engines since there was no service network which resulted into large losses for the company. In 1925 injector problems were mostly overcome and a new model, the F, was well received in the marine market. Next came the Model U with a new injection system. Clessie was after the car market, and in the 1920s with great difficulty he fitted a model 'U' four cylinder engine into a five year old Packard Roadster and drove it from Indianapolis to the New York motor show. Newspaper headlines ran - 'Startling demonstration. Diesel car - 35 miles to the gallon (US). In 1931 in the diesel class for the Indianapolis 500 race, a Cummins engined car was the only non-stop performer. At the same time, a Cummins engined truck drove coast to coast at a cost of 1 cent per ten ton mile of payload. In 1937 150 engines were being made a month as petrol engined trucks were sent in to be converted to the new 'economical power'. Some of you will remember the 85 FWD built timber tractors powered by the Cummins AA600 6 cylinder 100 b.h.p. engines sent over under Lease Lend in WWII. The company spread across the world and opened up here in Darlington in 1963 and Cummins made a deal with Chrysler Dodge then at Kew.

A friend of mine, Norman Tipping, became a test driver and knows about stop starts on a cabless ballasted chassis on nearby treacherous Zoo hill. He joined the dynamic Roots brothers Dodge, Commer, Karrier company when they started in Boscombe Road, Dunstable in 1954 where employees rose to approximately 1,800.

The Cummins V6 and V8 (up to 185 b.h.p.) with their patent fuel injectors were an option. This high 3000 revs engine had 3 colour bands on the rev counter, Green, Orange and Red, Orange being the recommended band. As for the prohibited Red area, get the needle here and you were really motoring!

Opposite over the road Bedford Trucks opened in 1955 on General Motors previous mid thirties site where repaired Churchill tanks had roared. I read from the press "In 1971 6000 employees produced up to 360 vehicles a day, claiming that theirs was a daily production larger than any other lorry maker in Europe. With poor factory security, Bedford and Roots workers, clad in similar overalls, would cross the road to see what models each other were producing and compare wage rises. Then came the crash. The name AWD still adorns the silent derelict factory, a brave takeover that failed in the early 1990s. Today Renault Trucks have a Parts Department of about 80 workers on the old Roots site and a smart Sainsbury supermarket stands on part of previous Bedford ground. The last British truck maker, ERF, has now succumbed. This century has seen the glorious rise and fall of the British lorry industry. Heavy haulage and timbermen have made mega demands on Horse, Steam, Petrol and Diesel power. They have often demonstrated how to gain unique power from engines never designed for such work loads.

Here in my village of Eaton Bray, Hawkins Transport, headed by Peter and son Jim, have a fleet of 11 ERFs, patriotically symbolised by a large Union Jack that flies in the yard. Very pro-Cummins, Jim speaks highly of the 400 model. Knowing the firm as I do, their name must feature with giants of transport. My criteria is not necessarily fleet size, but their standard of high customer satisfaction that must have brought them through the recession that crippled others.

'Clessie Cummins' invention now enjoys an increasing share of the market. Those of you that saw my video feature of the super giant 8 x 8 Unipower bridging vehicle demonstration, will remember my text on the proposed Tank Transporter version. Well its here, all 25 metres long of it, weighing 122-GCW tonnes, the heaviest goods vehicle of all time. Guess what? The MOD have chosen to power it with a Cummins QSK 19-750 HP turbo charged monster engine THAT EXCEEDS EXHAUST EMISSION CONTROL requirements, and generally powers Rail Cars. This mega vehicle has huge civilian potential as I predicted long before the commercial press (a Sanders first I seldom boast). If only Clessie, 'the man of ideas' was still around to observe the outcome of his diesel injection experiments, he'd have been proud indeed.

And finally, one aspect of the RTC is the effect beautifully restored vehicles have on old timber folk. Memories flood back, acquaintances are renewed and time stands still as they live it all again. I've heard so many stories start with - "I saw that tractor turn over" or 'I've seen her with 500 cube up' at so and so. A man said to me at Merrist Wood, 'Whose got that trailer over there, now?', pointing to a proud entrant. 'I towed her for years', he held forth on days when both he and the trailer were much younger. What's more exciting to turn up with a transformed old heap of twisted metal you've acquired, perhaps minus the wife's blessing, and restored it lovingly to its former glory, with scant knowledge of its history, to be approached by some old timer who'd pull out a faded snapshot with 'That's her when she was new and that's me at the wheel. What do you want to know about her?' It has happened many times. Just a year or two before his retirement, the Unipower Ben Hinton had learned to drive on at 16 years awaited him at our first rally. A crowd gathered as he demonstrated how to hand crank a 4 LW. This surely is what the club is all about. By the way, if you wish to measure the abundance of the owner's hobby, look round the low loader park and see how far those 40 foot tri-axle trailers have come. I admired Dick Oakey's ex TTB Foden in all her splendour, then shuddered to see his big transporter that he had brought in from Banbury. Others were from Essex, Somerset, Sussex, Hampshire, and so on.

In 1996 APF honoured the RTC with a sponsored stand at Europe's largest Forest Machinery Demonstration up at Telford, Salop. For three days, club members gave demonstrations of their saws and vehicles. Even John Bird of Marlow traipsed up there with his vast collection of old chainsaws.

In March 1997, APF News there is a page of a report taken from a German magazine, 'Forst and Technik'. There are just six photographs, five of VIPs and machines, and then of all the dozens of others they could have shown, there is one so familiar to us, the steam driven Rackbench saw, and it is captioned 'The Round Timber Club demonstrates how it used to be'. To be recognised in Europe within five years isn't bad going. Good luck to you all, you're doing a tremendous job.

In the RTC it is one of our jobs to display something of our great heritage, unbelievably dramatic as some of our situations seem in retrospect.

My visit to Merrist Wood brought me an invitation from RTC members Lyn and Trevor Johnson and family (see Chapter Five) to visit Newark where nearly sixty years ago I had joined the Army, spent two years' service, and met Helen. The photograph is of the Johnson family and me (on the left) taken when the visit took place in September 1997.

Four cylinder model Cummins 'U' Engine installed in 1920s Packard Roadster.

The RTCs first rally June 1992, Cranleigh, Surrey. A few of the 60 entrants.

Tony Maynarn, on the right, of Copthorne, Sussex moved this British Caledonian BAC3 fuselage at Gatwick. Previously used to train cabin crews it was relocated for fireman to practice crash rescues. Although lifted on by a giant crane, at 96 feet long and 16 feet wide, this was quite an assignment.

This is Paul Osborne's Fordson Super Major with Whitlock loading shovel, based at Bungay, Suffolk. He's adapted and fitted an ex-FWD Garwood winch with 200 yards of 3/4 cable and built on an anchor spade, P.T.O. driven (see inset).Since its linkage mounted the tractor front it bares down rather than rears up, "One hell of a winch", says Paul.

71

Helen and Maurice the proud owners pictured here of their first Unipower 'Hannibal',
WPE 795, in the mid-1960's.

Scores of these Latil 'trauliers' as the non-timber version was called, acted as tugs around
various docks

In 1924 a man named Riekie joined Latil UK and served as salesman, demonstrator and chief engineer. When Sir Nigel Gresley of railway fame approached Latil with an idea for a road-rail shunting tractor, this man designed and perfected the rail-wheel assemblies, drove the prototype down the Great West Road to the famous Firestone Tyre Factory and was cheered and filmed as this unusual tractor climbed the steps, went up on to the railway siding and on to the line.

Taken at Court Farm Shrawley, Worcestershire in 1933 when canvas appearing through the tyre tread was acceptable! (from Ben Hinton's collection)

THE NEW MOTORWAY

WE WERE THE CONTRACTORS FOR THE REMOVAL OF OVER 5,000 TREES FROM 55 MILES OF THE NEW MOTORWAY BETWEEN ST. ALBANS AND DUNCHURCH

Part of the timber ready for conversion   *Photo by H. Cooper & Son*

WE WERE SUCCESSFUL CONTRACTORS FOR THE SUPPLYING OF OAK GUARD RAIL POSTS FOR A, B AND C SECTIONS

STOCKS OF FENCING ALWAYS AVAILABLE AS SUPPLIED TO PUBLIC WORKS ROADS, ESTATES, AND LANDOWNERS. Quotations on request:

E. WHATTON & SONS

ENGLISH TIMBER MERCHANTS

HARTWELL   Telephone ROADE 233   NORTHAMPTON

A most interesting advertisement which appeared in the Northampton Independent in 1959. They don't stack them like this anymore. Reproduced by permission .

CHAPTER ELEVEN

Women at the Wheel

Readers of my previous books will know of my high regard for women in a timber man's world. As my back pain worsened my wife Helen came into tree work during her fortieth year. An astonished onlooker said "I've never seen a tart (then a term of endearment) fell a tree before.

In 1939 scores of scrapped cars were dumped in a 60 acre field just outside Eaton Bray as in other parts of the country to prevent German invaders landing their planes. It worked and the only successful invaders were spares-hungry motorists. In August 1947 an entrepreneur opened what he called a 'Sports Drome'. One attraction was the new fangled radio-controlled model planes that would fly off beyond range, landing in nearby cornfields which would be flattened as the owners searched for them. Hence an irate farmer would sit in the hedge with his gun and shoot them down as they crossed his airspace. In the top corner of this field today is a small industrial site that includes S and J Pierce transport, from where I'd heard of a lady HGV driver and husband going regularly across Europe.

I found Steve Pierce with a handful of radio phones. The answer was short and to the point; No, he had no photographs of either the lady or vehicle concerned. Then in a trice he was speaking to Jayne Dalton and husband Colin at the Milan depot in Italy. Could a photograph of Jayne at the wheel of the 1-8-97 Reg Volvo FH12 'Globetrotter' be taken? It was delivered to me by hand. Ex-van driver Jayne shares the rigours of European trucking with Colin on this all year round trip to Italy and back three times a fortnight. Leaving Northampton at 5am arriving in Milan between midnight and 3am, Channel Tunnel permitting. From driving a Bedford in the 70's to owning 34 trucks today is most creditable to Jenny and Steve as is their action of bringing you this photograph.

Sue Adlem is a part-time Library Assistant otherwise Sue is a relief driver on any one of Eric Choke's three 8-wheeled Mercedes Benz 340hp turbo bulk tippers, hauling aggregates but mostly sand, six days a week locally or delivering to Kent, Cardiff, Plymouth and countrywide. Her daily attire fluctuates between feminine dress or denims and Doc Martins dependent on the day's work. Hairy moments include climbing up out of a one-in-four slippy Kent chalk quarry with 20-tons on board. for ten years her husband Barry had driven for 80-year-old ex-land drainage contractor, Eric Choke of Billington near Leighton Buzzard, Beds.

Back in 1993 Barry felt that a regular, short-term (presumably male) relief driver was required. Little did he know that the successful applicant would be his wife Sue and that she would soon pass her HGV class one first-time, and load and work alongside the two other similar Mercs., bringing ladies skills into a male dominated world.

Nowadays, Barry determines the destinations of the 5,000 tons plus of sand etc moved every week, estimates the work, quotes and seems to be transport manager and service engineer all rolled into one.

Back in the 1960's Eric Choke and I featured on the same recommended Land Drainage List, but there the similarity ended. We lopped and felled to make way for drainage board draglines, whilst Eric had two Cat D6's, a giant Fowler, mole drainers massive tile laying machines and every form of water facility kits, thousands of pounds worth! Almost overnight, government policy decided against our own food independence and opted to pay farmers not to farm (but not contractors not to contract). Diversification led to concentration on sportsfield and golf course construction, etc.

As for Eric, his love lays with his well known gorgeous Burrell showman's engine which he still enjoys to rally. Here we have such trust and loyalty – let's savour it as there's not much of it around today.

I talked with David and Stephen Rodwell of Leicester Heavy Haulage with 20 vehicles including some abnormal load 150-ton units. They favour ERF with Cummins due to the "Jake" engine brake system. I hear Ilona Richards, secretary of The Lady Truckers Club was with this Leicester firm three years and drove both ERF and MAN 70-ton gross on air suspension outfits. She drove the length of the country, often away several days and nights with 16-feet wide cased materials to the docks.

Women today have an inherent knowledge of 'Wheel Womanship' passed down from their grandmothers in World War II. Those girls had but one instruction - 'Get there whatever'. I've seen bleary eyed lasses on Convoys driving 5 tonners with cargoes of food for stricken areas, forced to stop and get out to shift cables, rubble and tremendous obstructions to get through. I've seen a young lady ambulance driver, who might have squirmed at the sight of a dead mouse, mop up blood from her clothing and race off with a badly injured casualty in a crude box with rear tarpaulin curtains mounted on a cut back body of a requisitioned car, as so many were. I know about firewomen, undeterred by the dangers, drive water tenders into streets like vast blazing furnaces. These brave women were all victims of a war we never started. Small wonder their granddaughters are equal to the job behind the wheel of today's transport.

Giantesses (yes, there is such a word) of the wartime Women's Land Army, Land Drainage Section, with a typical dragline excavator. These girls played an important part in feeding us, when Hitler was set to starve this country out.

Drivers L/Cpl Dee Rix and Spr Sue Jefferies of Aldershot's TA 227 Amphibious Engineers Squadron who demonstrated this massive 3 metre wide, 400+hp, 34 ton laden, 8 x 8 Unipower at the treacherous Long Valley M.O.D. proving ground in December 1995. The vehicle and drivers met and exceeded every demand on this day.

Sue Adlem, part-time librarian and HGV driver (see text).

Jayne Dalton at the wheel of Volvo FH12 Globetrotters taken in Milan (see text).

Coming into the Docks is an abnormally wide load – typical of the type Ilona Richards drove. (see text). This inset photo is of Ilona.

Nichola's Nightmare: the Rev. Nichola Jones pictured with the author and who with HGV driver Sylvia Dominey carried out a Girls Sponsored Truck Drive on this 10 feet wide 25 ton Mighty Antar tow truck, which raised over £3,000 including the sales from the subsequent video. (September 1990.)

A MAN OF PRINCIPLE

My publisher's father, Bert Gurney, was employed by Sainsbury's in Luton in the late 20's and early 30's, but was sacked because he refused to work on a Sunday, being a strict Sabbatarian. With millions unemployed it was very difficult for him to obtain another job, and with two young children had to look much further afield. He came to work as a Corn Merchant's manager in the out of the way village of Ashwell, in Hertfordshire. This interesting picture above shows him with a delivery van in the 1920's, in the days when Sainsbury's came to you. We often glibly say: "It's a matter of principle",. So did this man and really meant it.

MILITARY GIANTS

This section is all photographs, one from World War II, the rest either being current military vehicles or ex-military vehicles now privately owned.

Giants of War. The business end of a M25 Pacific 6 x 6 armoured 'Dragon Wagon' Tank Transporter. Biggest vehicle in World War II. 12¹/₂ ft wide x 63 feet long which required 1 gallon of petrol per quarter of a mile. Note the 60,000lb Garwood winches and chain and sprockets of the rear drive. My encounters in London with this mega monster are still vivid, 53 years on. Convoys of these 'freedom fighters' for you and me, were seen making for Slapton Sands Devon prior to D-Day. Courtesy Bart Vanderveen.

This is a British built Alvis Unipower Tank Transporter that will carry 75 tons of tank at 50 mph coupled to a French Nicolas Trailer (65% made in UK) with 6 rows of 4 wheels, the last 4 of which steer, making for ideal cornering. Nineteen litres worth of Cummins power pack also drives the twin 25-ton capacity winches and completes this mega machine. Let's wish it well on its current multi-continental sales tour. This is really a big 'un. The Renault 5, which belongs to photographer Shaun C. Connors, proves just that.

An earlier picture in Chapter 11 (Women at the Wheel) shows the TA girls who here are putting the 34-ton loaded 8 x 8 Unipower through its paces at the Long Valley, Aldershot proving course, in 1995.

This vehicle, a 6 x 6 High Mobility Load Carrier has been designed and built as a one off by the MoD funded Defence Evaluation and Research Agency, to meet the demands of varying terrains. This 'test bed' for state-of-the-art automative technology incorporates a Cummins L10-350 E11 engine. (Photo: Shaun Connors.)

The Stalwart in the mud hole was taken at a quarry in Avon Dassett. Twice yearly, like-minded enthusiasts gather to play with their ex-military hardware in the type of terrain it was intended for.

This beauty has been re-engined with a Rolls-Royce Eagle 220. This was another Shaun C. Connors photograph, (as above) and taken at Bovington, in a similar get together as at Avon Dassett.It did come through, by the way!

The majestic "Foden 8 x 8 also going through its paces at a trial ground (Photo Shaun C. Connors.)

Now lads here is typical wartime situation for this double-jointed Scammell Explorer in difficult terrain. They certainly do not make them like this anymore. (Photo: Shaun C. Connors.)

CHAPTER TWELVE

The House of Healing

On 17th December 1996 I took my usual half hour walk, returned for a meal, snoozed and drove my car in the afternoon. I awoke next morning quite unable to stand on the powerful legs that had taken me high in the trees for forty years and void of all ankle feeling save acute leg 'pins and needles'. My doctor came, telephoned a consultant who visited me and concluded a hospital assessment was required. The outcome was to be twenty-seven visits made twice weekly to St Mary's Day Hospital, Luton. Here a day of selected exercises and various therapies are given. About thirty outpatients are transported in by ambulance crews who appear to have degrees in T.L.C.!

My first view of this group of Alzheimer, Parkinson and stroke victims had me thinking arrogantly: "Surely I've not come to this"! but I was to realise these people were really only a little further down the road I am travelling. I met folk who knew the real meaning of pain, suffering and permanent disability and had the privileged friendship with some who put my problems into perspective. Fellow ex-servicemen's experiences enthralled me as we delved into memories of World War II over coffee. One 88-year old lady said of us: "They're busy winning the last war still". A special rapport and banter exist between staff, particularly ambulance crews and patients. It seems one of the perks of ageing is unlimited permissible gentle verbal sexual harassment, the female of the species being the worst.

A lady with an ample bosom was having her seat belt fastened with care to avoid touching, only to say: "Don't worry about my erogenous zones, that's what we come for"! This and lots of other incidents would bring forth roars of laughter from four elderly ladies nicknamed 'The Golden Girls'. I name them Lily, Grace, Edith and Jean (the mischievous one). I've heard them laugh with gusto, and shriek with pain. I know too of the sobering loneliness that awaited return to their homes. They taught me lessons in bereavement no counsellor could match. Their courage is indescribable!

An ambulance crew of three, Mary, Phil and Tony, worked two vehicles: the single driver for walking patients whilst the other two would share the driving. One was kept busy checking addresses, keeping an eagle eye on all, particularly on a middle-aged

84

Alzheimer sufferer who continuously undid his seat belt and needed regular saliva wiping. Others would be sick occasionally or feel ill. I saw great acts of human kindness from the crew members.

I always thought there were just two kinds of ambulance drivers. Those on the light-flashing siren-sounding 'Blood Wagons' and others with the snip job of out-patient pick up. How wrong I was! These immaculately turned out crews have a vast understanding of human nature, a wealth of compassion and a high standard of professionalism for which we, as a society, pay them 'peanuts'.

Every member of St Mary's staff from domestic to consultant are highly skilled and positively conditioned with a happy sense of healing that prevails in this place, dedicatedly managed by Sister Newson, who excels in this branch of medicine. Dealing with demands of an ageing population calls for a state of almost saintliness, displayed daily by members, who smile with encouraging words yet must be screaming on the inside.

After introductions, my physiotherapist, a brilliant young woman named Cathy, with smiling eyes and an infectious laugh, wheeled me away to face her latest challenge. Her added burden was having to put every instruction on to my mini tape recorder due to my amnesia, the invisible affliction.

My now much-pained, degenerative spine reminds me of the day in 1962 when a gust of wind had taken me down from a tree to twenty feet below, to land onto a branch previously cut. I recall being lifted into the back of my Land Rover, lying with a sack for a pillow, ankles over the tailboard with chainsaw etc thrown in round me. At home my doctor saw no need for an X-ray but recommended work as soon as possible to prevent permanent stiffening. It was Bart's Hospital which discovered three crushed vertebrae fractures five years later after new backache which developed after a big bulldozer started pushing a large Elm top onto a fire, unaware I'd just started cording up within. Battered and bruised, I extricated myself with some difficulty.

A geriatric C reg Ford Transit ambulance that had given such faithful service and 104,500 miles and had two replacement engines, had a gearbox as indecisive and as clapped out as its cargo. It darted around picking up patients. (Now it has been replaced with a new Iveco vehicle.) Memories flooded back from the 1950s on, as we visited one location after another. One pickup was right next door to a house where an extension had made access to the rear garden possible only via the kitchen and ornately-furnished front room through which I wheeled a complete sawn up elm tree via some 60 barrowfuls, when a log rolled off just missing an antique china cabinet!

Just off Drovers Way, Dunstable, was where the MET Office was then situated, and had sent that crucial D-Day forecast on June 1944.

Nearby I'd topped out a beech tree and recalled spilling a half tin of 'Arborex' tree wound paint on my mate down below. Using petrol with a water rinse, a new kind of 'Wash and Go', we removed the sticky gunge.

We passed the three-acre site we'd cleared for the council where we'd been continuously pestered by local residents about future plans. One frustrating day an annoying, persistent enquirer was told in a confidential whisper that a 'Helicopter Pad' might be a possibility! A deluge of Council officials arrived in no time and their anger was not easily abated.

Elsewhere and on another occasion, I'd agreed to fell a dead ash for a fiver whilst clearing a building site. The County Forestry Officer slapped a T.P.O. on it, saying "I need to see if there is any green on it in the spring". My comment that any green on it would have to be paint upset him. In the meantime, a bungalow was built below and it cost £50 for me to rope it down limb by limb. Reminders of my halcyon days awaited me in many places.

On Tuesday, 29th April 1997, I walked reasonably well through the door I'd been regularly pushed through for four months, thanking the staff and God as I did so. This coincided with my publisher inviting me to attempt a further project, at a time when I couldn't even write a shopping list, let alone a book. But slowly, as my body miraculously returned to some semblance of normality, I felt moved to try and put something back on behalf of those of us who have benefited from Doctor Mylvaganam and his splendid team. Therefore all the royalties of this book are destined for The St Mary's Day Hospital Fund that supplies many additional needs.

There was a line in a TV sitcom about an Old People's Home when an inmate greeted a newcomer with "Welcome to God's waiting room". Such homes are occupied by some whose current memory fails as fast as older experiences can be recalled. I'm not alone in being able to reel off my army number yet cannot recall my postcode. Cathy, my physiotherapist, urged me to walk always with my drooping left shoulder held up. A quite impossible task without Helen to constantly remind me. The answer came in the form of a good daub of paint on the back of my hand, exposed whenever I reach for my stick. For some reason this leads to roars of laughter from folk who can think of no better ideas of reminders. One quite concerned nurse wondered if it was a skin condition; she's been in dermatology and questioned "It's not just ordinary paint, I hope?" I replied, "Oh no, it's Tractol, John Deere Green - 100% rustproof too." I bet she'd not read about that in 'Nursing Mirror'!

Looking back on what some of you will see as a scrapheap of humanity, some will deride quite rightly the world we have left you. But, as we are always being told, we must be positive. Among the proud patients at St Mary's are a microcosm (a posh word I like to use) of folk of their day. A breed that first as fellows and girls gave five or six years of their peak twenties that you may continually use the phrase 'It's a free country', with little thought of how it became and is kept so. True, we've not cured unemployment and, 'the Devil finds work for idle hands' crime-wise. Instead, we've brought you the computer, a mixed blessing that puts thousands out of work at the touch of a key. Across the board, education-wise, many now reach a standard previously only enjoyed by the well off. The hours you work mostly bring a higher standard of living than those who worked about as long again. Scores of fair rights have been won, and the planes we developed for war, now updated, whisk you across the world in forms of travel undreamt of. We brought you the 'Swinging Sixties' which swung rather a lot one way, bringing sexual freedom in the extreme; from which molestation of women and children is now traced. So much so that in years to come, tracing who sired whom will be quite impossible for the would-be family tree tracer, devastating much of `family life' of pre-war times, accompanied by depths of unhappiness and misery.